# Modern Mindfulness

How to Find Peace and Happiness in a Busy World (2nd Edition)

Wil Dieck

**TMT Publishing**

Copyright © 2023 by Wil Dieck

All rights reserved. No part of this publication may be reproduced, distributed, or transmitted in any form or by any means, including photocopying, recording, or other electronic or mechanical methods, without the prior written permission of the publisher, except in the case of brief quotations embodied in critical reviews and certain other noncommercial uses permitted by copyright law.

Thank you for your support of the author's rights.

TMT Publications

ISBN: 978-1-956169-09-6 (Hardback)

ISBN: 978-1-956169-05-8 (Paperback)

ISBN: 978-1-956169-06-5 (E-book)

Wil Dieck wil@mindfulmindhacking.com San Diego, CA

## Limits of Liability and Disclaimer of Warranty

The author and publisher shall not be liable for your misuse of this material. This book is strictly for informational and educational purposes. Warning – Disclaimer: The purpose of this book is to educate and entertain. The author and/or publisher do not guarantee that anyone following these techniques, suggestions, tips, ideas, or strategies will become successful. The author and/or publisher shall have neither liability nor responsibility to anyone with respect to any loss or damage caused, or alleged to be caused, directly or indirectly, by the information contained in this book.

Copyright © 2023 Wil Dieck

# Contents

| | |
|---|---|
| Acknowledgments | 1 |
| Forward | 2 |
| Introduction | 3 |
| 1. Finding Peace in a Busy World | 5 |
| 2. The Origin of Mindfulness - Meditation | 9 |
| 3. What is Mindfulness? | 14 |
| 4. What Mindfulness Isn't | 20 |
| 5. Some More Advantages of Mindfulness | 23 |
| 6. Doing Mode vs. Being Mode | 31 |
| A Sincere Request | 37 |
| 7. The Principles of Mindfulness | 39 |
| 8. Mindfulness and Mindlessness | 45 |
| 9. Emotional Awareness | 50 |
| 10. How to R.A.I.N. on Difficult Emotions | 54 |
| FREE Guided Meditation Course! | 56 |
| 11. Developing Helpful Attitudes | 58 |

| | | |
|---|---|---|
| 12. | Learning to be Non-judgmental | 61 |
| 13. | The Difference Between Meditation and Mindfulness | 65 |
| 14. | Is Practicing Mindfulness Meditation Worth It? | 68 |
| 15. | The Importance of Living in the Present Moment | 73 |
| 16. | Mini Mindfulness Practice in Daily Life | 76 |
| 17. | A Life filled With Distractions | 79 |
| 18. | Tips for Rapid Improvement | 83 |
| 19. | Dealing with Problems and Distractions | 87 |
| 20. | A Beginner's Guide to Relaxation | 91 |
| 21. | Belly Breathing | 94 |
| 22. | Practicing Mindfulness | 98 |
| 23. | Mindfulness in Daily Life | 102 |
| 24. | Mindful Focus - One Step at a Time | 107 |
| 25. | Therapeutic Mindfulness | 112 |
| 26. | Mindfulness and Social Psychology | 115 |
| 27. | How to Use Mindfulness | 119 |
| 28. | Tips for Fitting Relaxation into Your Life | 125 |
| 29. | Daily Mindfulness Exercises | 128 |
| 30. | Body Scan Meditation | 131 |
| 31. | Guided and Non-Guided Visualization | 136 |
| 32. | Mindful Breathing | 142 |

| | |
|---|---|
| 33. Progressive Muscle Relaxation | 145 |
| 34. Mindful Walking | 148 |
| 35. Conclusion | 152 |
| About the Author | 154 |
| Other Books by Wil Dieck | 155 |
| Endnotes | 156 |

# Acknowledgments

I am incredibly grateful to everyone who has contributed to this book, but in particular I want to recognize those who have been truly instrumental in its completion. Finally, there are many others who have helped me academically, in martial arts, and spiritually; you know who you are, and I thank you immensely!

My partner Lynette Seid is a constant source of love and motivation. Thank you from the depths of my heart for your constant encouragement.

To my two wonderful children Vanessa and Samuel Dieck: you both inspire me to be better every day.

To my late parents Arne and Lealia Dieck: you will always be an inspiration for me to become the best version of myself.

To all my dear readers: thank you for taking the time to read this book – it was created with you in mind.

# Forward

When I first wrote Modern Mindfulness, my goal was to write a book that laid out the basics of mindfulness meditation.

When I finished, I felt I had accomplished my goal, then I took on other projects and wrote other books.

Since then, I've had feedback from many readers who told me that, although they were happy with the content, they wished the book was less academic and had more exercises.

In this 2$^{nd}$ edition, I took their feedback to heart and took off my professor's hat and, hopefully, wrote it so it was easier to read.

I also incorporated more easy-to-follow exercises you can use to develop your mindfulness practice.

I hope this edition will not only introduce you to the joys of mindfulness meditation but also enable you to enhance your practice as you read through it.

I hope you'll share your adventures with me.

My email is Wil@MindfulMindHacking.com

Best wishes to you on your journey!

Wil Dieck

January 2023

# Introduction

"Be happy in the moment, that's enough. Each moment is all we need, not more." - **Mother Teresa**

MINDFULNESS MEDIATION HAS BEEN with us for thousands of years. It is an ancient practice that has been used to improve our spiritual, mental, and physical well-being.

In fact, tens of millions of people practice mindfulness meditation daily worldwide. They do this because they find it very helpful to improve their well-being, while giving them a greater sense of fulfillment and happiness.

How it helps to achieve these, and more, is the subject of this book.

While I don't pretend to be a "Mindfulness Guru", for over 40 years I have practiced Mindfulness in my daily life, and I've practiced even longer as a martial artist.

I believe that practicing mindfulness meditation has transformed, and probably even saved, my life.

After leaving the military in the mid-1970's, I was on a self-destructive path filled with substance abuse and the type of highly detrimental behavior that accompanies it. That is, until I was fortunate enough to re-encounter martial arts and begin on my mindfulness journey.

In the ensuing years, practicing mindfulness has changed me from that substance abusing maniac spinning rapidly out of control into a calm, at least most of the time, focused loving father, friend and teacher devoted to improving my life and the lives of those I encounter.

It has also helped my concentration, focus, and discipline, which, I hope, comes across in this book.

I wrote this book to help anyone understand the basic concepts of mindfulness while giving some easy-to-follow methods you can use to practice mindfulness in your everyday life.

Now that's enough about me.

Let's get back to what you can expect.

In this book, we're going to dive somewhat deeply into the world of mindfulness meditation. We'll also demystify the information that sometimes surrounds it.

Let's start by examining why it's so important, especially today, to find peace in a busy world.

# Chapter 1

# Finding Peace in a Busy World

"In the end, just three things matter:

How well we have lived

How well we have loved

How well we have learned to let go"

—— **Jack Kornfield**

Today, more than ever, everyone is busy. In fact, being busy is something we all take for granted. Many wear it as a badge of honor.

Take a moment and think about people in your life.

Can you think of anyone who isn't running around trying to juggle careers, school, and home life? Anyone who isn't busy all the time trying to fit in and succeed?

This busyness fills our lives with tension and uneasiness. The pressure of it all can become enormous.

How can anyone handle all this while keeping their sanity?

You could try meditating mindfully.

Of course, mindfulness meditation is nothing new. It is an art form practiced by people from around the world for millennia.

For the past few decades, there's been tons of research conducted on the benefits of both mindfulness and meditating. This research shows these ancient practices can help calm our minds and slow things down, something nearly anyone can benefit from today.

## Our Busy World

Today, rushing is something everyone does.

You rush off to work. You run home to make dinner.

Then there is homework, laundry, and dishes. After that you feed the dog–or cat, and the kiddies. Then there are those few things you'd like to finish before going to bed.

Examine the tools you carry. Even if you work in the trades, you have a smartphone. Everyone has one of those these days.

If you work in an office, you probably also have a tablet or laptop or both.

These tools make you available for your work, your friends, and your family to contact you, anytime and anyplace. This is fantastic if there is an emergency.

But how often are you contacted for an emergency? Usually, these devices are electronic leashes that you simply can't get away from.

Even in the car, you are busy doing something with one of these tools. Today, cars have hands free devices that allow you to chat, make appointments, or even close business deals.

How convenient, but also how annoying. You, like your devices, are always on.

Years ago, you could escape by taking the bus or train. We used to even view it as a restful experience.

Not today.

These devices just follow you around, demanding your attention no matter where you are. There is wi-fi on buses, trains and even airplanes.

There isn't one place your mind can get any down time if these devices are on. And we don't turn them off, do we?

When was the last time you turned off your devices for 24 hours? How about 12 hours, 6 hours or even one hour?

How about 15 minutes?

If you did it at all, it was probably because your device ran out of juice because you forgot to charge it. One more thing to stress you out!

And you wonder why you feel so burned out.

This is where mindfulness meditation can help.

## Slowing It All Down

Practicing mindfulness meditation gives you time to slow down and relax. Whether sitting on the floor or in a big comfy chair, closing your eyes for 15 to 20 minutes and focusing on just one thing can be a tremendous help.

This practice gives your body and mind time to relax and take a break. To let your mind stop thinking at a million miles per hour.

It can help you feel glad to be alive again.

Practicing mindfulness has helped millions of people from around the world learn how to calm their minds. It does this by teaching you to pay attention to one thing at a time.

As you learn to focus your mind, you'll notice that your concentration has increased, along with your productivity levels. You'll be accomplishing more work in less time, leaving time for more important things, like your relationships or hobbies.

On top of this, you'll start enjoying life again!

So, if this is what you want to do, this book can help.

Let's get started!

# Chapter 2

# The Origin of Mindfulness - Meditation

*"Exercise, prayer, and meditation are examples of calming rituals. They have been shown to induce a happier mood and provide a positive pathway through life's daily frustrations."* - **Chuck Norris**

STUDIES SHOW THAT MINDFULNESS can help to reduce anxiety, depression, pain and, as I mentioned above, even help with issues like substance abuse. It is also a way for a person to develop their spiritual being.

According to Mindful.org, "Mindfulness is the basic human ability to be fully present, aware of where we are and what we're doing, and not overly reactive or overwhelmed by what's going on around us." [1]

It is the meditative practice of paying attention in a calm, focused manner.

Before we dive deeper into mindfulness, let's visit its roots, meditation.

The best guess is that the practice of meditation existed even before recorded history. Historians estimate the first Indian civilizations practiced meditation as long as 5,000 years ago.

Over 2,500 years ago, the Hindus wrote about meditation in the Vedas. The Vedas are the original scriptures of Hindu teachings that contain spiritual knowledge said to encompass all aspects of life.

Ancient Hindus used meditation as part of their path to awakening and enlightenment.

But Hinduism does not have a monopoly over meditation as a practice. Ancient records link mindfulness and meditative practices to Taoism in China and Buddhism in India and Japan.

Christianity, Islam, Sikhism, and Judaism also have meditation traditions and techniques.

Buddhists were the first to formalize the practice of meditation in India about 2,500 years ago. It was Gautama Buddha, the founder of Buddhism, who first used formal meditation practice to establish an organized approach to enlightenment.

They captured these practices in their scriptures. These writings explain a person reaches "Nirvana", which is the ultimate spiritual goal of Buddhism, by meditating.

From India, this practice spread into Tibet. An Indian sage named Bodhidharma finally brought it to China. Here he eventually founded the Ch'an school of Buddhism at the Shaolin Monastery. This school is better known in the West by its Japanese name, Zen.

We'll examine some of these meditative practices more deeply throughout this book.

## Describing Meditation

Here's an easy way to think about meditation. It is a practice that simply allows a person to train their mind to have more disciplined thinking. This type of thinking can assist a person in having a better outcome.

For example, maybe you spend a lot of time thinking about mistakes you've made and how your life might be better if you hadn't made them. Practicing mindfulness can help you stop ruminating over the past and just let things go. It can also help you develop the type of mindset that focuses more on positive than negative events.

By practicing mindfulness meditation, you can learn how to relax your mind and body. Buddhists and Hindus believe this can help you develop a new life force, called gi, ki, or prana.

At a practical level, meditation can help you learn how to love again, have compassion, open your heart, and forgive. It can also help you open your mind to new opportunities.

Many religions incorporate meditation into their beliefs.

Buddhist monks practice meditation daily. It is central to performing nearly all their rituals.

Using things like prayer beads, meditating helps these monks keep track of things that they want to accomplish. Touching the beads also focuses their minds on mindfully saying their mantras. These mantras, or repetitive sounds, are used to help the practitioner keep their mind calm and focused on the present moment.

## Why Meditate?

Meditation is often used to help clear your mind and get your body and mind working together in sync.

The goal is to relax your mind and notice your thoughts and feelings. You accomplish this by focusing your mind on one thing at a time.

The things you might focus on are endless. While you could simply focus on your breathing, you could also focus on things like losing weight or forgiving someone for a recent slight or an action they took that disturbed you.

Researchers have found that there are many ways to practice meditation and its practice can provide many benefits. Again, this can be everything from improved concentration to better relationships.

Taking part in yoga is another way to meditate. Some people meditate while kneeling or sitting and repeating phrases or quotes. You can even practice mindfulness meditation while walking, which can be a powerful method for calming your mind in a busy world.

Religious practices often had strict guidelines and expectations for someone meditating, depending on their background. However, today, how you practice meditating is a personal choice.

The biggest thing to keep in mind is finding a location and position that is comfortable for you. One that allows you to practice somewhat undisturbed.

Now that you have a basic understanding of meditation, let's dig a little deeper into mindfulness.

# Chapter 3

# What is Mindfulness?

*"Mindfulness is deliberately paying full attention to what is happening around you– in your body, heart, and mind. Mindfulness is awareness without criticism or judgment."* – **Jan Chozen Bays**

I WAS FIRST INTRODUCED to the word mindfulness in the early 1990's when one of my martial arts students told me about Jon Kabat-Zinn's book, "Full Catastrophe Living".

You might have had a similar experience, learning about mindfulness from a book or story in the media. Maybe a friend told you she started practicing mindfulness at the local community college.

No matter how you heard about it, you probably picked up this book because you were curious about what mindfulness is and what it can do for you. This is a great place to start.

What does it mean to be mindful?

Think of it like this. As a child, your parents probably told you to "pay attention".

What they were telling you was to be aware of what you were doing and how it was affecting other people, usually them. This is a good starting point for understanding what mindfulness is about.

Mindfulness is about paying attention to what is happening right now, right before your eyes. It also includes being aware of any other thing that your other senses can perceive, including your internal or spiritual senses.

We derived the word mindfulness from the word sati, which signifies attention, awareness, and remembering. This awareness is a spiritual or psychological quantity that forms an essential part of Buddhist practice.

Over the years, psychotherapy has modified the definition of "mindfulness" to fit its use as meditation adopted by CBT. CBT is 'cognitive-behavioral therapy' and is a very successful psychotherapeutic approach for treating many psychological conditions like anxiety, phobias, addictions, etc.

Mindfulness is a tool CBT therapist have adopted that you too can use not only to reduce your stress and calm your thoughts but also aid in your ongoing self-improvement.

One of the most important ways it does this is by helping you to focus your awareness. Being able to focus your awareness is intrinsically powerful for your psychological wellbeing.

Becoming more aware of what is occurring around and within you allows you to unravel the negative thoughts and feelings that preoccupy you. Understanding these thoughts and feelings helps you live a calmer, more productive life.

It does this by helping you guide your attention to the information your body is providing you with and putting you in touch with your thoughts.

Here are a couple of examples.

What tensions and pains are you experiencing in your body right now?

How is that making you feel?

What are you thinking about right now?

Are you even aware of what you are thinking about or are you, like most people, on automatic pilot, daydreaming, or maybe going over and over a difficult encounter that happened a day, week, month or even years ago?

One of the biggest challenges of focusing on past events or worrying about the future is it can pull you into an unproductive state.

For example, depression is often associated with replaying past events in your mind. Stress and anxiety can result from worrying about future events.

Like most people, much of your thinking is not in the present. But the present is the only time you've got.

This is how practicing mindfulness helps. It keeps you in the present because your life is simply a series of present moments.

If you continually return to negative past events or imagine catastrophic future ones, you will become stressed and anxious. There's just no getting around it.

By learning to move your life more into the present moment, you can relate to the past and the future differently. You can see them through a new lens. This helps to soften their effects.

As you find these thoughts easing, you discover living right here and right now is where you want to be, because you feel more vibrant and alive. Life takes on a whole new meaning.

Most people who have been practicing mindfulness for a while will tell you they have regained energy that, in the past, they used to waste fighting off anger and sadness. They'll also tell you that their minds have become calmer, more focused, and clearer.

Before we continue, let's start off with a simple mindfulness exercise.

Note: If you are reading this to learn mindfulness, then I recommend you DO this exercise.

Choose a small everyday object that you don't hold an emotional attachment to. For example, a coffee mug, lamp, cell phone, pen, etc. Stay away from photos of people, animals or even a plant that you might have any feelings towards.

1. Visually examine the object without touching it for 2 minutes. Note what you see.

2. Describe the object without judgement. For example, instead of saying it is 'small' say it is 'about an inch in diameter'.

If you find it helpful, write what you notice on a piece of paper. Here are some things you might ask yourself:

- How does the surface appear?
- What's its shape?
- Does it appear solid or does light pass through it?
- Is it straight, curved, or a combination of both?
- Does it appear shiny or dull?

- Do any shadows cross it?
- Does it have any reflections on its surface?
- What color(s) and shade(s) does it have?
- Does it look smooth or bumpy?
- Does it appear to be soft or hard?
- Is it wet or dry?
- Is there anything else you notice about it?

3. Next, hold the object in your hands and feel the object for 2 minutes. You might find closing your eyes enhances your sense of touch while doing this.

Here are some things you might notice:
- Does it feel hard or soft?
- Is it smooth or rough?
- is it sharp or dull?
- Does it feel rigid or is it pliable?
- How heavy is it? Note: Describe it as a measurement, such as "6 ounces" or "about a pound".
- How cool or warm is it? Note: Choose a temperature such as "70 degrees Fahrenheit".
- Does it feel different in particular areas as you move your hands over it?

Think about your experience.

Did you notice anything new/different by focusing on a common object in this way?

How easy or hard did you find it to concentrate on the object?

As you examined the object, did you feel any emotions? If you experienced emotions, did you hold on to or reject them?

Excellent!

You have just completed the first mindfulness exercise in this book. It introduced you to what it feels like to be mindful.

This exercise illustrates that mindfulness is not about escaping reality and living in a fantasy world. Instead, it is becoming present.

You are discovering how to live in this moment.

Mindfulness is about where you place your focus.

As you found earlier, this is more relevant today than ever.

We keep getting distracted because we have created a world filled with stimuli competing for our attention. As these stimuli simultaneously attack our senses, we become stressed and anxious.

As you use mindfulness, you learn to stay focused. This helps you calm your mind and concentrate on what is most important at this moment.

This is the magic of mindfulness. Helping you maintain your focus, keep your calm, and get more done.

These are just a few of the advantages of mindfulness. We'll look at more later.

Now let's look at what mindfulness isn't.

## Chapter 4

# What Mindfulness Isn't

*"Stop, breathe, look around and embrace the miracle of each day, the miracle of life."* - **Jeffrey A. White**

MINDFULNESS ISN'T ABOUT BEING perfect or competing with others. It isn't just about meditating, and it doesn't require a lot of time or effort to practice. Mindfulness isn't about stopping your mind from thinking, and it isn't about escaping reality either.

In short, mindfulness is for everyone, regardless of age, background, or beliefs.

Mindfulness is all about being present in the moment and paying attention to your thoughts, feelings, and sensations without judgement.

It's about connecting with your innermost self and learning to accept yourself as you are.

It's about slowing down and savoring life instead of rushing through it, taking time to pause and appreciate the world around you and within you.

Mindfulness is an opportunity to open to a new way of being that can bring peace, energy, purpose, joy and clarity into our lives.

Here's what mindfulness is not:
- Spending time thinking about the world and all the wonders you can find in it
- Contemplating the great, deep mysteries of life
- Some magical practice that brings good luck into your life
- A spiritual practice reserved only for those in highest connection to their Creator and can dedicate hours to every day
- Daydreaming or fantasizing about what your perfect life looks like

## Mindfulness is NOT Mystical

Yes, meditation and mindfulness in the modern world may have some of these mystical connotations, but mindfulness is much simpler.

In simple terms, mindfulness and meditation are ways to achieve a calmer state of mind. Mindfulness is essentially a sub form of meditation.

Although mindfulness originated with non-western practitioners ages ago, today it's practiced and studied by scientists, psychologists, and doctors all over the world.

So, if you're ready to bring more mindfulness into your life and see the world from a different perspective, this could be the start of a beautiful journey

Hopefully this gives you a better idea of what mindfulness is.

Now, let's look at some more advantages practicing mindfulness brings.

# Chapter 5

# Some More Advantages of Mindfulness

*"Mindfulness gives you time. Time gives you choices. Choices, skillfully made, lead to freedom."* –**Bhante Henepola Gunaratana**

MINDFULNESS IS VERY BENEFICIAL for many aspects of life, from pain and disease management, to sleep, to physical health and control of emotions.

A study published in Nature Human Behavior[2] identified mindfulness as an effective mental health practice for helping almost anyone improve their physical and psychological well-being. The study also found that practicing mindfulness can positively affect a person's mental health.

With this in mind, let's look at some advantages of practicing mindfulness.

**1. Mindfulness helps lower stress.**

In today's world, it's easy to be triggered by people or events. These triggers can set off your fight-or-flight response, or your body's reaction to a perceived threat.

This fight-or-flight response, also known as the acute stress response, can cause you to feel anxious and stressed. Left unchecked, these increased stress levels can lead to both physical and mental health issues.

They can also interfere with your personal and professional relationships.

Mindfulness is not only associated with feeling less stressed but is also a link with decreased level of cortisol, or the stress hormone[3].

**2. Reduces levels of depression.**

Too much stress can lead to depression. One of the most important benefits of mindfulness is it can help relieve symptoms of depression.

While it can help anyone, specific studies have found that practicing mindfulness lowers depression risk among pregnant women and teens.

Both pregnant and post pregnant women can suffer from depression. Studies show that practicing mindfulness yoga has a link to reducing these feelings and may help prevent these symptoms from returning in the future.

It can also help to lower depression risk among teens. Studies show that teens taught how to practice mindfulness experience less anxiety, stress, and depression.

Other research published in the Lancet[4] suggests that a combination of mindfulness and cognitive-behavioral therapy can reduce depressive symptoms and help prevent a relapse of depressive symptoms as effectively as antidepressant medications.

**3. Helps regulate emotions.**

Triggers can also cause emotional outbursts. These flare-ups can cause both personal and professional problems.

For example, you may like your job and enjoy working with your co-workers. One day you find a co-worker looking in your desk drawer without asking first.

With a deeply furrowed brow and accusative voice, you angrily ask her what she was doing in your drawer.

She leans away from you as she meekly replies, "I just needed a post-it for my report," then turns and hurries back to her desk.

As she goes back to her desk, you realize that your emotions have gotten out of control. Not only do you feel bad, but you are also concerned that your co-worker might avoid you from now on or you might even lose your job.

All because you let your emotions get the better of you.

Practicing mindfulness helps you regulate your emotions. This regulation comes in part from being able to help you identify your feelings. Once you can identify them, you can learn to control them.

**4. Nurtures relationships.**

Mindfulness can also be good for your relationships "by bringing open, non-judgmental attention into the interactions with people around us."

A 2018 study[5] showed mindful people were more accepting of their partner's flaws and imperfections. It does this by allowing us to accept our partner's shortcomings instead of focusing on their flaws and trying to improve them.

Another benefit is as we become better able to accept our partners, we become more satisfied with our relationships.

**5. Helps boost memory.**

Have you ever misplaced your keys or forgotten where you put your cell phone? Maybe you've forgotten you had to pick up your kids and then had to rush to school, only to be cross-examined why you were so late?

These types of minor memory problems can turn into a major annoyance and result from a phenomenon known as proactive interference. This phenomenon happens when older memories impair newer ones.

In a 2019 study[6], participants either took a creative writing course or received four weeks of mindfulness training. In tests of short-term memory, those trained in mindfulness practice showed the greatest reductions in proactive interference.

**6. Increases brain flexibility.**

Some people worry about their ability to focus. One very consequential benefit of practicing mindfulness is it trains your mind to be more capable of holding attention for extended periods. It also is beneficial for cognitive flexibility.

Mindfulness is exercise for the brain. Since its practice is about learning to be more aware of your thoughts without imposing judgments on them, it makes sense that practicing mindfulness can help you think more clearly.

Studies[7] found that mindfulness can help you focus your attention. It allows you to stay focused, even with lots of distractions. It can also help suppress thoughts that interfere with your focus.

These cognitive abilities are very helpful for a wide variety of everyday tasks. For example, increased focus helps you concentrate on what you're working on. You can use this concentration for improved problem solving. It also makes it easier for you to switch from one undertaking to another.

**7. Mindfulness helps you sleep better.**

One of the more significant benefits of mindfulness is it can help you sleep better. [8]. While many people turn to pharmaceuticals to help them sleep, mindfulness offers a better long-term solution without the side effects.

Its practice is also associated with lower brain activation at bedtime. It does this by targeting multiple cognitive/emotional processes that contribute to poor sleep quality, like ruminative thoughts and emotional reactivity.

It also helps you see your daily experiences from a different perspective. All these factors can contribute to better sleep.

**8. Improves physical health.**

Scientists have discovered that mindfulness techniques help improve physical health in several ways. It helps by improving body awareness, relaxation skills and stress management.

Mindfulness can help relieve stress. It has been used to help treat heart disease and lower blood pressure. It can also reduce chronic pain and ease gastrointestinal difficulties.

Not only does mindfulness help improve health, but it also reduces the risk for a variety of illnesses. One study found "mindfulness brings about various positive psychological effects, including increased subjective well-being, reduced psychological symptoms and emotional reactivity, and improved behavioral regulation.[9]"

Of course, this can help lower your health care costs. A study found that practicing Transcendental meditation resulted in lower yearly doctor or co-pay costs because it helps you to stay healthy.

**9. Mindfulness protectively changes the brain**

Integrative mind-body training is a meditation technique. This type of mindfulness meditation can bring about brain changes that may be protective against mental illness.

One way it does this is by working as the brain's "volume knob". Mindfulness helps the brain have better control over processing emotions and pain. It does this by regulating the cortical alpha rhythms, which control what senses the mind is attentive to.

By helping you control these rhythms, mindfulness works with you to help control your emotions. This can make it easier to cope with your feelings.

Over time, this can help to improve many areas of your life, including your personal and professional relationships and overall feelings of well-being.

A review of several studies concluded that "mindfulness brings about various positive psychological effects, including increased subjective well-being, reduced psychological symptoms and emotional reactivity, and improved behavioral regulation.[10]"

This has a positive effect on mental well-being by helping you develop healthy thought patterns instead of getting stuck ruminating on negative thoughts. This positive focus can help improve your mood and help you feel better overall.

As you practice mindfulness, you'll learn to let go of the past and not worry about the future. Living in the present reduces stress and worry.

As discussed before, practicing mindfulness may also reduce some symptoms of anxiety and depression.

A study published in Frontiers in Human Neuroscience[11] looked at the effects of practicing mindfulness on anxiety, depression, and rumination. They found it not only had positive effects on their anxiety, depression, and rumination, but also improved their overall emotional states.

Overall, mindfulness practice can help you learn to better regulate your emotions. Its practice can also aid you in becoming more calm, patient, and empathetic.

**10. Mindfulness lets you become more self-aware.**

Mindfulness will help you objectively analyze yourself so you can get to know yourself better. This self-awareness is a path to becoming a more enlightened person, although not like what you see in movies or read in books.

Instead, it helps you by giving you a better understanding of why you do what you do. This understanding allows you to forgive your mistakes and the mistakes others might make as well.

Another benefit of being more aware is it helps you conquer common "blind spots" that can hold you back from becoming a complete and whole person. When you realize how these blind spots are affecting your progress, you become motivated enough to take the action necessary to overcome them.

**11. Improves academic success**

Mindfulness is effective in helping students achieve academic success in any age group.

College students who practiced mindfulness perform better at reasoning problems. They also experience improvements in their working memory.

Teenagers who took part in a mindfulness program while studying for a general education certificate[12] experienced lower depression and anxiety. This contributed to their improved academic success.

Elementary students taught to practice mindfulness[13] exhibited greater pro-social behaviors and emotion regulation. This helped them achieve higher academic performance.

So, if you, or someone you know, want to improve their grades, mindfulness can help, no matter how young, or old, you are.

**12. Mindfulness helps you even when you are not actively practicing and helps you become a better person.**

A study has established that the amygdale brain region's response to emotional stimuli is changed by meditation. The study concluded that mindfulness meditation "also led to increased functional connectivity between the amygdala and a region implicated in emotion regulation.[14]"

This was even when a person was not actively involved actively in a meditative session.

People who practice mindfulness are also more compassionate and exhibit more "do-good" behaviors.

As you can see, there is a lot of evidence that shows the positive effects of mindfulness on your mind, body, and spirit.

Hopefully, this evidence has convinced you to continue reading and practicing what you'll find in this book.

Now, let's look at the difference between doing and being.

# Chapter 6

# Doing Mode vs. Being Mode

> *"Mindfulness is simply being aware of what is happening right now without wishing it were different; enjoying the pleasant without holding on when it changes (which it will); being with the unpleasant without fearing it will always be this way (which it won't)."* – **James Baraz**

THE PROCESS OF LEARNING to drive can be overwhelming for a beginner. One must focus on keeping the vehicle between the lines while at the same time watching traffic signals, road signs and other cars.

You must also constantly glance at the speedometer to see to it that you are driving at a safe speed.

Doing all these is not easy because you must also concentrate on what may be happening on the highway. You must also watch out for animals and pedestrians depending on where you are driving.

As you gain driving knowledge and experience, it becomes more and more of an automatic process.

It becomes so automatic that at some point you can take a routine drive without remembering anything about it. Sometimes your mind can wander so much that you miss a turn or an exit.

This is what the process of automatization is all about. Automatization occurs in many areas of our lives and can occur without our conscious awareness.

Thoughts and feelings can also become automated in a way that you find yourself having a strong emotional reaction to a situation without knowing why. This would mean that one of your automatic emotional processes got activated.

Mindfulness is the opposite of this automatic pilot experience. This is because it involves paying attention to your immediate experiences without falling into automatic patterns of reacting and behaving.

Mindfulness is a shift from "doing mode" into "being mode". Let's start by examining the doing mode.

## Doing Mode

Here are some examples of the doing mode:
- Being aware how things "are" and thinking about how they "should" be.
- Being goal-oriented and constantly trying to fix things.

- You continue to put in more and more effort into reaching your goals.
- You are not consciously aware of the present moment.

In the doing mode, most of the actions you take tend to happen automatically.

Let's look at the example of what you do in the morning.

Suppose you were in the shower. Was your mind really with you in the shower or did it keep on racing from one memory to another?

Were you smelling the fragrance of the soap and feeling the warmth of the water on your skin? Were you hearing the sound of the water?

Probably you were not.

When you are preoccupied with thoughts of getting things done, or with thoughts of the past or the future without giving attention to the present, then you are in doing mode, or "thinking mode".

This is because for you to get things done, you generally have to think about those things first. The doing mode takes you away from experiencing the world directly with your senses.

Once you leave the doing mode and focus your awareness directly on the information provided by your senses, you have entered the "sensing mode".

This is what mindfulness awareness teaches. It teaches you to focus on the world that you experienced directly with your five senses: smell, touch, sight, hearing, and taste.

As you experience life in the sensing mode, you are introduced into a richer, more colorful world.

You will never feel bored or pathetic if you treat each experience as if it is happening to you for the first time.

Such an approach is said to be having a "beginners mind" or a "child's mind".

## Being Mode

Here's what happens in the being mode:
- You are connected to the present moment.
- You acknowledge how things are right now, in this moment.
- You have a willingness to allow things to be just as they are instead of trying to change what's happening.
- You accept pleasant, neutral, and negative emotional states realizing they are all a natural part of life.
- You have a sense of calmness, stillness, and a feeling of being centered.

Before examining what the doing mode consists of, do the following visualization exercise. It will help you get in touch with your own being mode.

Imagine you are sitting by the ocean.

Feel the breeze blowing over you.

As you imagine the ocean, notice that the surface of the ocean is full of movement. The waves may be choppy, or they may be peacefully rolling into the beach.

Just look at and observe the waves.

Be aware of how they move, how active they are.

Now imagine that you go out into the ocean until you are in deep water.

Allow yourself to sink down, deep into the ocean water.

As you sink down, you are looking up from the deep, still water below.

You see the choppy surface above you.

From down here, you can cultivate a calm and quiet awareness.

Just relax and enjoy this sense of being.

A still and quiet place where you simply are.

Observing the world from a place of peace.

Give yourself a few moments to enjoy being here and then come back to the here and now, so that you can examine the being mode more fully.

## Back to the Being Mode

The being mode nourishes your mental state. It creates the time and space needed for you to experience joy, right now, in the present moment.

By remaining in the being mode as much as possible you become more mindful.

The benefits of being mindful are associated with decreases in levels of avoidance, rumination, self-delusion, maladaptively and perfectionism.

Let's quickly define these terms.

Avoidance means to refuse to accept the reality of a given situation.

Rumination is the condition of being trapped in negative thought cycles.

Maladaptively self-delusion, on the other hand, means attempting solutions that maintain the problem.

Perfectionism means attempting to control a situation.

In the "Being Mode" or "Sensing Mode" these negative behavior patterns and thoughts are reduced and quieted. In this mode, you allow yourself to become fully aware of what is going on around you and within you, without attempting to manipulate or control these sensations and events.

The being mode allows you to detach from your emotional and cognitive processes so you can stop them, or observe them, if you choose.

Mindfulness aspires to cultivate the being mode, allowing things to be as they are already. What you'll find over time is, when you stop trying to change things, they change by themselves in ways that are both beneficial and amazing to you and the world around you.

You'll discover how to move into the being mode, and more in this book. But first, let's look at the principles of mindfulness.

# A Sincere Request

Dear Reader,

Thank you for picking up my book.

Hopefully by now you're beginning to get some good use from it. The upcoming chapters will have even more mindfulness exercises for you to work on.

I hope you realize how much your support as a reader is appreciated by me as!

As an independent writer and publisher, I do not have the budget or publicity to help promote my books. So, I am asking you for a favor.

If you have been enjoying this book, please consider leaving a review to let other potential readers know why you decided to pick it up in the first place.

Your feedback would also be a great help to me in improving what I write in the future.

To leave a review, simply scan the QR code or click on the Amazon link below:

https://www.amazon.com/dp/B0BS8VPMHN

Any feedback is incredibly helpful and much appreciated!

Adding your two cents will go a long way in benefiting not only me, but also other readers like yourself.

If you have any questions, please visit my website at https://mindfulmindhacking.com/contact and contact me directly.

Thanks for your time!

*Wil Dieck*

# Chapter 7

# The Principles of Mindfulness

> *"People usually consider walking on water or in thin air a miracle. But I think the real miracle is not to walk either on water or in thin air, but to walk on earth. Every day we are engaged in a miracle which we don't even recognize: a blue sky, white clouds, green leaves, the black, curious eyes of a child—our own two eyes. All is a miracle."*- **Thich Nhat Hanh**

I DIDN'T BEGIN FORMALLY studying mindfulness until after I read Jon Kabat-Zinn's book, which had an introduction from Thich Nhat Hanh. Before that, I had dabbled in studying Zen Buddhism and Taoism. While I don't consider myself an adherent to either of these religions, I appreciate how studying them widened my perspective.

After I began studying mindfulness, I found its principles are largely based on Buddhist or Zen principles. Over the years, I have found that mindfulness practitioners from many walks of life have found these principles to be helpful in developing their internal balance.

Because mindfulness is a discipline, I recommend you practice contemplating the following principles in different situations as you navigate through life's twists and turns.

These principles include:

**Awareness**

Being aware is a choice. To notice what is present, you must first choose to be aware. This is the only way you can become comfortable with its existence.

Trying to avoid whatever you feel is uncomfortable, or "checking out" is counterproductive. Awareness is about committing to maintaining conscious awareness of your internal experiences, or "checking in".

**Present-moment focus**

Practicing mindfulness is about prioritizing the present moment. This is counter to most people's thinking.

One thing that makes your mind so amazing is it can quickly go in different directions. In an instant, it can look to the future, revisit the past, or be in the present. It can solve analytical problems or examine abstract notions, all within a moment in time.

While each of these has important roles in your life, in practicing mindfulness, your awareness needs to prioritize the present moment. This involves cultivating the ability to tune into sounds, sights, thoughts, physical sensations, and emotions that are occurring right now.

**Acceptance**

Once you are aware of what you are experiencing, you can learn to accept that it is true.

This does not mean that you must like it or that there isn't a better way for things to be. It only means that you are acknowledging the present reality without trying to change it or fight it.

**Non-judgment**

The mind usually categorizes experiences as right or wrong, good or bad. As you experience something, you'll probably say something such as, "I like it" or "I don't like it."

From very early in life, your parents, teachers, siblings, and friends have helped to condition you to react like this. It's a hard habit to break.

But it is also possible for you to observe and describe your thoughts, sensations, or feelings without evaluating them.

This is very similar to how scientists look at and then review data. They simply watch and record data as it appears, then evaluate it later.

This is what non-judgment is all about. This principle is about having curious interest and attentive observation about what's happening instead of judging or evaluating.

You are simply accepting things as they are.

**Validation**

This principle assumes that whatever you are experiencing internally is valid, and it is there for a reason. You don't have to understand the origins of an experience or your reaction, you simply validate it.

This is how you come to peace with it.

As you notice emotions, thoughts, or physical sensations, instead of looking for its genesis, you assume your reactions are valid based on your personality, genetic predisposition, or learning history.

This allows you to cultivate an attitude of validation.

**Tolerance**

As you tune in to your internal experiences, you may find that some of them are unpleasant or cause pain. As this happens, instead of trying to change or block them, allow yourself to experience the sensation.

This principle helps you cultivate tolerance for things that make you feel uncomfortable or cause you pain. This can be helpful in many situations.

For example, tolerating the negative feelings that come up when working through emotions. Athletes have also used mindfulness to increase their pain tolerance and speed up their recovery process.

**Compassion**

When we make an error or do something without thinking, a common reaction is to criticize ourselves. But would you do this to a friend who is suffering because they made a mistake or did something unfortunate?

Probably not.

Just like the response you have for a friend who is in pain, suffering can help you develop compassion toward yourself.

For those of us who have developed a habit of self-criticism, this principle can feel quite foreign. But it can become a powerful healing experience as you learn to cultivate an attitude of self-compassion.

### Invitation

If you notice you have an old habit that is not serving you well, you may decide that it is necessary to revise it.

Perhaps you find that your mind is clinging to anger, or your body is holding on to tension. Instead of scolding yourself to let go of the feeling and change it, you gently invite your mind and body to be open to new possibilities.

Think of this as if you were trying to get a child to do something. What happens if you say, "stop doing that!" There's a very good chance that the child will continue or even escalate their behavior.

Alternatively, if you said, "Maybe you could try doing this instead", the child might be more willing to try the behavior you suggested.

The principle of inviting a change will often lead to more willingness. Trying to force a change creates resistance.

### Patience

When have you experienced the most discovery and growth? It's probably when you have had to develop a skill that took time and patience.

Having to go through a learning process can feel painstakingly slow. This can be especially true as you are learning to practice mindfulness.

As you already know, change is hard. Allow yourself to cultivate an attitude of patience toward your progress. As Saadi once said, *"Have patience. All things are difficult before they become easy"*.

### Practice

All the above principles can inspire and enlighten you. However, unless you decide to put them into practice, they are just an entertaining intellectual exercise.

As the saying goes, a seed that is not planted will never grow.

The same goes for your mindfulness practice. For your mindfulness to grow, you must make a commitment to practice what you have learned.

The only way you can reinforce these principles and cultivate your peace of mind and body is to practice.

One last thing.

There may be other concepts and terms that apply to your practice of self-awareness, consciousness, and personal growth.

Add them to the above list and then change them to suit your preference.

Before we move on, let's do another exercise.

Take two or three minutes and brainstorm and what you think the opposite of focus is.

I'll answer this in the next chapter.

Don't peek!

## Chapter 8

# Mindfulness and Mindlessness

> *"One does not become enlightened by imagining figures of light, but by making the darkness conscious. The latter procedure, however, is disagreeable and therefore not popular."* —— **C.G. Jung**

TO INTEGRATE MINDFULNESS INTO your daily life, you need to experience it. The best way to begin is to learn mediation from an experienced teacher. Your teacher can provide you with both direct experience and a conceptual road map to guide your practice.

While the definition of mindfulness, which can be awareness, experience, and acceptance, is easy to remember, its direct experience can be tricky. Sometimes it is easier to understand it by examining its opposite.

## The Opposite of Focus

At the end of the last chapter, I asked you to brainstorm ideas about what you think is the opposite of focus.

I hope you did the exercise. This is because the exercises you'll find throughout this book can help you become more mindful. As with any skill, the only way to become better is to practice.

So, what is the opposite of focus?

From a mindfulness perspective, the opposite of focus is called 'default mode'. Neuroscience calls this the default mode network (DMN), which is a system of connected brain areas. When someone is not focusing on what's happening, the DMN shows increased activity.

This is our normal mental state. In this state, the mind wanders from one thought to another. This state is like the commercial that shows a dog sitting patiently by his owner when a squirrel appears. Then you see the dog's thought bubble "say" squirrel and the dog runs after it, dragging its owner.

This is the default state. Like the dog, in the default state, our minds get distracted easily.

Here are some examples.

You are working on a project on your computer and need to check a reference online. As you check, a story about a famous person appears and, after reading the headline, you click the link to the story. Ten minutes later, you find that you've not only read that story, but three others as well.

You're talking with a coworker, and she tells you about a vacation she took in Mexico. As she's telling you the story, your mind wanders off, thinking you need to leave a little early for lunch today because it's Taco Tuesday.

You're driving to work, and you hear a song on the radio that reminds you of a time when you were a teenager. You think about the good times you had with your friends long ago and wonder where they are now. Then you notice you missed your turnoff about five minutes ago.

These are all examples of the default mode, where the mind wanders as one thought leads into another.

You are living mindlessly. This is your typical mental state.

You, like most people, spend most of your time lost in fantasies of the future and the memories of the past. You're operating on "autopilot". Your mind is in one space and your body is in a completely different one.

Often, you'll try to escape the present moment by rushing to get to the "good stuff".

You hurry through the dishes so you can watch your favorite television program. You zip through a conversation so you can begin reading your newest novel.

Most of the time, you rush through whatever you are doing to get rid of as much of your life experience as possible. All without paying attention to what you are doing at this moment.

Even now, as you read these sentences, where has your mind gone?

Has it strayed?

Are thoughts like, "I wonder if this book is going to be worthwhile," meandering through your mind?

Maybe your mind has left this book entirely. You're thinking of what you will do later, or what you're going to eat for dinner.

Perhaps you're thinking about something that happened to you yesterday or earlier today.

This is not a bad thing per se if the thoughts are neutral or positive. Sometimes it can even lead to a creative process.

But this isn't good if we focus on negative images, things we can do nothing about.

Sometimes this happens when we worry about one thing and then have one negative thought after the other. We ruminate, imagining all the negative scenarios possible, and make ourselves more and more worried.

Sometimes, we can start perceiving stressful occurrences that are not even real. Events that just exist only in our imagination.

Now we're stressed over nothing at all when we don't need to be.

The persistence of everyday mindlessness is very striking when you really think about what's most important in your life.

Take a moment to recall a time in your life that you really valued.

Perhaps it was time special time you had with a loved one.

Maybe it was a magical experience in nature.

As it was happening, where was your mind? While you were there, did you spend your time imagining the future or recalling the past?

Most probably not.

Odds are that it fully focused you on that very moment. Your mind stayed present without wondering off to the past or future.

The moments you value the most are those in which you are fully present, noticing what is happening there and then. These are the moments of mindfulness.

Like in the exercise, you notice your hands and their position. You're in tune with the sensations of holding whatever you have in your hand, as well as everything happening around you.

When you're driving, you are aware of your body sitting in the car. You are aware of other cars, the road, and the scenery.

When you eat, you chew your food and taste the food. You deeply experience the sounds, sights, and others around you.

Mindfulness involves being present in your life.

When you honestly reflect on the state you are usually in, you'll notice that most of the time you are in a mindless state. You are not being present with what's happening in your life.

The mindless state will bring you to a point where your mind is no longer your own.

As a result, you can become a mindless savage or zombie.

Later in this book, you'll see how mindfulness can help you deal with this, but first, let's examine how you can become more mindful of your emotions.

# Chapter 9

# Emotional Awareness

*"Above all, we cannot afford not to live in the present. He is blessed over all mortals who loses no moment of the passing life in remembering the past."* - **Henry David Thoreau**

EMOTIONAL AWARENESS IS THE ability to recognize, understand, and appropriately express your emotions. It involves understanding why you feel a certain way, being able to communicate these feelings to others, and responding effectively in challenging situations.

Emotional awareness helps us to better understand ourselves and our relationships with others, enabling us to make healthier choices and build stronger connections.

## The Importance of Emotional Awareness

Having emotional awareness can help you maintain a healthy balance between expressing your needs and respecting those of others.

As you become more aware of how your emotions affect your decisions, behavior, and interactions with those around us, you'll be better able to manage difficult emotions. This will allow you to respond calmly instead of impulsively or emotionally.

With practice and dedication, you can nurture emotional awareness, develop emotional intelligence, and create a healthier life for yourself.

## Mindfully Practicing Emotional Awareness

Learning to become emotionally aware takes time and practice. You can start by taking regular moments to pause and check in with yourself.

Ask yourself, "How am I feeling at this moment?"

Once you've identified your emotions and understood where they're coming from, you can then decide how to respond and take action if needed. With time and patience, you can learn to use your emotions as a powerful compass to guide you through life.

Let's examine a simple process that can help you become more mindful of your emotions.

**Know the feeling is present**

You become emotionally aware when you know feelings are present in you and others.

This is the first level of emotional awareness.

You notice the feeling when you first think about it or realize that you feel something in that moment.

**Acknowledge the feeling**

After you noticed, for example, a person, you might acknowledge them by saying hello or by waving. You can do the same for a feeling.

While you may not know exactly how to define a feeling, by noticing and acknowledging that you have a feeling, you're closer to identifying it.

**Identifying the feeling**

Once you know a person is near and recognize them, you can greet them by name. You identify them.

In a similar way, you can identify and name your feelings.

Be as specific as possible so that you identify your feelings. The more accurate you are in identifying an unmet emotional need, the better you can take some appropriate action.

**Accept the feeling**

After identifying and greeting a person by name, you can then move to help them feel accepted.

The same also happens with emotions.

Once you have identified it, you can benefit from the natural value your emotions bring you by accepting the feeling.

Of course, we're already discussed the benefit of acceptance earlier.

**Reflect on the feeling**

The time it takes for you to feel your feelings to identify them is nearly instantaneous. But emotional awareness requires that you reflect on the feeling as soon as possible.

The sooner you reflect on the feeling, the sooner you can take action.

**Forecasting feelings**

By becoming mindful of your current emotions, you can understand what triggers certain reactions. This allows you to predict what will happen if certain events or scenarios play out down the line.

For example, if you know that a certain person makes you feel anxious whenever they enter a room, then you can take precautions when they're around to avoid feeling that way.

You can improve this ability by considering how you will feel if you choose one course of action over another. Your prediction of a positive feeling can help you make it happen.

In the same manner, your prediction of negative feelings can help you avoid doing something you believe will prevent it from happening.

Predicting emotions isn't always easy. Our minds and hearts are complex, and how we experience the world will often shift without warning. But if we take the time to reflect on our experiences and note how different emotions like insecurity or hope have shaped our lives, then we can gain insight into how similar events may affect us again in the future.

When we acknowledge our feelings, both positive and negative, we create space for understanding. This allows you a better chance to make more informed choices in life.

Next, you'll learn a simple mindful process to help you move through your difficult emotions.

# Chapter 10

# How to R.A.I.N. on Difficult Emotions

*"You cannot control the results, only your actions."* -
**Allan Lokos**

LIFE CAN BE TRICKY at times. As you learned in the chapter on emotional awareness, we all experience difficult emotions and stressful moments, but with mindfulness, we're equipped with a set of tools to help us better handle these situations.

One tool you can use when you experience difficult emotions, such as anger, fear, or frustration, is R.A.I.N.

**R--Recognize what is going on.**

When negative emotions arise, take a deep breath, observe your body, and mind, and ask yourself—what am I feeling right now?

**A--Accept it as it is; allow.**

This doesn't mean that you have to like the uncomfortable emotion, but rather that you let it be as it is. You don't have to resist it or fight it, just acknowledge its presence.

**I--Investigate the physical sensations, thoughts, and feelings.**

Spend some time exploring the different aspects of your experience. Focus on the physical sensations in your body, the thoughts running through your mind, and the emotions arising within you.

**N--Non-identification.**

Remember that you are not defined by your emotions, you are bigger than your negative feelings. Acknowledge that you are having an emotional experience but remind yourself that this passing emotion does not define you.

By using the framework of R.A.I.N., you can learn to better recognize your emotions. Instead of getting lost in those negative feelings, you can use mindfulness to be more present with your experience and create space for acceptance and understanding.

Now, let's examine how to develop more helpful attitudes.

# FREE Guided Meditation Course!

**CONGRATULATIONS ON BEGINNING YOUR Mindfulness Journey!**

By reading "Modern Mindfulness: A Beginners Guide on How to Find Peace and Happiness in a Busy World," you've taken an important step toward greater peace, clarity, and happiness—even in the midst of a hectic life. Now, why not continue your journey with a powerful next step?

We're excited to offer you a FREE Guided Visualization Course, designed just for readers like you.

**Why Try This Course?**

**Build on Your New Mindfulness Skills**: Visualization is the natural companion to mindfulness—helping you turn peaceful awareness into real-life transformation.

**Easy, Guided Practice:** No experience needed! You'll get simple, welcoming sessions that show you how to use visualization to create calm and joy in your daily life.

**Fits into Any Schedule**: Short, practical lessons work with even the busiest routines.

**Completely Free:** No strings attached! Just a genuine gift to support your next step toward lasting happiness and well-being.

You've learned how to be present, now discover how to shape your future with the power of your imagination.

Join the Free Guided Visualization Course Here

or follow this link – https://blackbeltbreakthroughs.com/a-beginners-guide-to-guided-meditation/

or scan the QR code below.

Let's build your peace, one gentle step at a time.

You're ready!

Don't wait any longer.

Start your meditation journey today!

# Chapter 11

# Developing Helpful Attitudes

*"Mindfulness meditation doesn't change life. Life remains as fragile and unpredictable as ever. Meditation changes the heart's capacity to accept life as it is."* -
**Sylvia Boorstein**

ONE DEFINITION OF AN attitude is "our assessment of ourselves, other people, ideas, and objects in our world." Attitudes are important because they affect both our perception of the world and our behavior.

This is the importance of incorporating the following mindful attitudes into your daily life. They help fashion your perception of the world, which influences the way you behave.

These basic attitudes about mindfulness are interdependent and each can influence the degree to which you can cultivate the others.

It also can often be best to work on only one of these attitudes at a time.

Let's examine them now.

**Beginner's mind**

This attitude prevents you from getting stuck in the rut of your expertise and allows you to be receptive to new possibilities.

With curiosity, you can see things with a fresh viewpoint, just as if you are seeing them for the first time.

**Non-judging**

A non-judging attitude is an impartial observation of your experiences. You do this by not labeling feelings, thoughts, and sensation as right or wrong, good, or bad, etc.

The habit of judging and categorizing your experience can lock you into mechanical reactions instead of present awareness.

This attitude is so important that there is an entire chapter on it in this book.

**Patience**

Patience reminds you that things unfold in their own time.

This is a smart attitude. Patient openness to each moment is helpful to invoke when the mind is wondering or agitated.

**Trust**

In practicing mindfulness, you are practicing taking responsibility for learning to trust and to listen to your own being, and for being yourself.

Trust your own inner goodness, your intuition, your own authority, and your own wisdom, even if you make mistakes along the way.

**Non-striving**

A non-striving attitude means you are not trying to get anywhere other than where you are.

Remember, meditation is non-doing.

Most of what we do should make us progress or get us somewhere and improve. A non-striving attitude is, therefore, the polar opposite of how we live.

**Acceptance**

Acceptance describes the embrace of the deep and true understanding of how things really are.

This is not the passive acceptance of the intolerable and is not resignation or giving up.

Acceptance is a pause, a period of letting be, of allowing, of clear seeing.

**Letting go**

Mindfulness is an invitation to let things to be as they are so we can have a fresh perspective of every moment.

We hold on to things when they look pleasant and conjure them up again and again.

But when they feel unpleasant, we avoid them.

These attitudes need to be cultivated in a way that supports your mindfulness practice.

Remember that mindfulness does not just appear by itself without effort. If you have decided that the practice is good for you, you must commit to its practice.

As you persevere, you will develop a higher degree of mindfulness.

To help you, let's dive a little deeper into one of the harder to adopt attitudes, learning to be non-judgmental.

# Chapter 12

# Learning to be Non-judgmental

> *"Somewhere in this process you will come face-to-face with the sudden and shocking realization that you are completely crazy. Your mind is a shrieking gibbering madhouse on wheels barreling pell-mell down the hill utterly out of control and hopeless. No problem. You are not crazier than you were yesterday. It has always been this way and you just never noticed. You are also no crazier than everybody else around you. The only real difference is that you have confronted the situation they have not."* - **Bhante Henepola Gunaratana**

WE ALL MAKE JUDGMENTS, it's human nature. Over many thousands of generations, our minds have developed the ability to judge quickly and easily.

The reason it does this is to "keep us safe". While this can be an excellent thing in an emergency, like when being attacked by a grizzly bear, they can throw us off track, or even "make us crazy" as Bhante Henepola Gunaratana points out.

How do we make judgements?

We make judgements based on our own experiences and our world perspective. They originate from our own moral compass, values, beliefs, stories and understanding, which come from our own life experiences.

Social scientists tell us they first come from our parents, siblings, teachers, and peers. Later, they result from our work experiences, personal relationships, people we learn from, as well as those we interact with.

Of course, today this includes media and social media.

All this contributes to creating different thoughts and feelings about us and the world. This is how we develop our automatic internal responses.

Every moment your senses, sight, hearing, tactile feelings, taste, and smell take in information that causes your brain to be triggered. Using this information, your brain will decide if this is something "normal" and safe or abnormal and potentially dangerous.

Again, this can be great if you are approached by a Hell's Angel you are not familiar with in a biker bar, but not so great when approached by the new person in your work area.

Our recent experiences and feelings also affect our judgements.

For example, if we have had a good night's rest, we have more tolerance, acceptance, and patience. But if we're at the end of a long, stressful day, these might all fly out the window.

If judging is automatic and negative, how can you overcome its influence on you?

You can use mindfulness.

Using mindfulness to identify how you judge things.

Find the following images in a web search.

A cute, small animal.

A person looking out a window.

Horse flies.

A woman resting on the beach.

Butterflies

An older, well-maintained car.

Look at each image for 60 seconds.

Quickly note what comes to mind about each image.

Did you judge these images in any way?

For example, was the image pleasant or unpleasant, good or bad, calming or distressing, etc.?

Take only 30 seconds for each image to write your judgements.

Next, without judgement, just describe what you see.

For example, of a color, you can say 'yellow' instead of 'bright yellow' or 'two butterflies' instead of 'pretty butterflies.'

After you finish, take about 5 minutes to determine how it felt. Was it different from your first experience of the image?

This exercise helps you to remove your judgmental attitude. Stepping back this way allows you to become more detached from preconceived ideas and emotions.

Don't confuse detachment with being selfish or not caring. It also does not mean to avoid reality.

In fact, as this exercise showed, nourishing a non-judgmental attitude encourages you to be more in touch with reality.

This attitude allows us to let go of ideas, objects, and people that make us suffer or do not let us see other perspectives or other points of view. If we get too attached to our judgments or preconceptions, they can prevent us from expanding our horizon.

One purpose of mindfulness is to allow us to let go while staying aware. You have an awareness that something exists, such as a feeling. Mindfulness lets you examine it uncritically and decide to let go.

For example, as you try to focus, you find that other thoughts or emotions are entering your mind. Instead of trying to suppress them, you notice them. If they are not important right now, you can choose to let go of them.

This is how you can use non-judgement to improve your life.

Now that you have a better understanding, let's look at the difference between meditation and mindfulness.

# Chapter 13

# The Difference Between Meditation and Mindfulness

> *"Do every act of your life as though it were the very last act of your life."* —— **Marcus Aurelius**

MINDFULNESS IS A MENTAL quality or state. In this state, you focus your awareness on what's happening in the present.

Meditation is an intentional practice you can use to develop distinct qualities, like calmness, concentration, awareness, and emotional balance.

Meditating requires more of a break in your day because it calls for attention and concentration. Its intention is to connect the mind to the body so you can find mental and physical peace.

For example, many types of meditation, such as transcendental meditation, instruct you to think of 'absolutely nothing'. To do this, meditation instructors will often direct you to focus on your breathing, a mantra, or a physical object like a candle flame.

The problem is this focus is often difficult for beginners to achieve. This is because they, like everyone else in the world, will find their mind wandering constantly, making them feel frustrated.

Mindfulness meditation isn't about trying to empty your thoughts. Instead, its goal is to help you step back from your thoughts and 'observe' them like a scientist or a detached third party.

This way, you aren't letting your thoughts affect you, causing you to feel stressed or frustrated. Your mind isn't struggling with not being 'allowed' to think about anything.

One advantage of using this technique is it allows you to become more aware of your own thought patterns. This awareness gives you the ability to edit any patterns that are leading you down a troublesome path.

Let's say you find you have a nagging, constant feeling that something bad is going to happen to you. Practicing mindfulness allows you to notice this habitual thinking pattern. Now that you've recognized it, you are better able to find thoughts you can replace it with.

This may be the long-term aim of mindfulness when used with Cognitive Behavioral Therapy.

In the short-term, though, you can simply use mindfulness to step back from your thoughts and emotions. This allows you to gain some of the mental space needed to examine and calm those thoughts. Now you can recover your focus and get ready to tackle the day ahead.

Before moving on, let's revisit the object focusing exercise from the chapter explaining what mindfulness is.

Remember, unlike meditation, mindfulness isn't about directing your attention and concentration to connect your body and mind. While this can be a byproduct of mindfulness, it is more about being present in the moment.

It is about directing your focus.

Think back to the object focusing exercise.

Hopefully, as you examined the objects with your eyes and hands, you noticed something new.

This is the magic of mindfulness. It helps foster curiosity.

The attitude of curiosity motivates you to focus on the small things in life. Being curious allows you to appreciate life more.

This heightened awareness helps you find joy in everything you encounter.

This is like the attitude children normally have. Everything is new. The world is full of surprises. Everything seems amazing.

As we grow older, we stop seeing all the wonderfulness there is in the world. We take things for granted.

Through focus, mindfulness can help us rediscover that lost sense of wonder.

But there are even more reasons to practice mindfulness. This is what we'll examine next.

# Chapter 14

# Is Practicing Mindfulness Meditation Worth It?

*"The mind is just like a muscle - the more you exercise it, the stronger it gets and the more it can expand."* - **Idowu Koyenikan**

MOST PEOPLE WON'T START something new unless they feel compelled. They must have a reason that moves them to act.

It's just human nature. We all want to get results from our efforts.

This is probably true for you, too. To help you decide, let's highlight some reasons becoming more mindful can be beneficial.

## 3 General Categories

The benefits of mindfulness fall into three categories: therapeutic benefits, mental benefits, and benefits that help improve your well-being.

Therapeutic benefits are those that aid people in resisting the effects of things like anxiety, depression, pain, and schizophrenia.

Mental benefits include increased stability of the mind and self-understanding.

Well-being benefits include feeling healthier and having more energy.

Let's look at these general areas, one at a time.

**Therapeutic benefits of mindfulness**

Depression, stress, and anxiety are rampant today. These are just a few examples of the mental issues that mindfulness can help soothe.

If you have a feeling of anxiety or feel jittery, then mindfulness practice can help. If you regularly experience some uncomfortable body sensations such as butterflies in the stomach or sweaty palms, then mindfulness can help here as well.

You feed your anxiety when you ruminate over negative thoughts. These thoughts can keep your anxiety alive and, over time, cause it to rise.

Using mindfulness, you can change your perspective about these thoughts. This change of perspective allows you to take a step back from them, giving you more control.

Likewise, by mindfully examining your anxious feelings, you can learn to dial them down and make them tolerable. You can even learn how to calm them altogether.

Your difficulty with panic and anxiety often results from body sensations, such as a churning stomach or a pounding heart. Using your mindful awareness, you can identify these symptoms for what they are–physical sensations.

By understanding the underlying issue, you can use mindfulness to reduce their effects and ease your symptoms.

While health professionals often prescribe medications, these only mask the symptoms. They don't address the underlying issues.

Instead of trying to cover up the symptoms, mindfulness changes your attitude about the symptoms. It does this by accepting and embracing them, rather than fighting them and pushing the symptoms away.

When you use mindfulness to examine them, even your thoughts simply become thoughts you are currently having, not something to be believed uncritically. Also, your emotions become part of your current experience, something to be examined, not pushed away.

Mindfulness helps embrace the richness of fully feeling sad by realizing that even powerful emotions like anxiety are not all that bad when you view them simply as the body sensation of some tightness in your stomach.

You can also use mindfulness this way to reduce stress and ease pain.

**Mental benefits of mindfulness**

Mindfulness helps make you more mentally flexible and balanced. It also improves your concentration.

It can help you become more self-aware, leading to a clearer understanding of your own mental processes.

For example, have you ever found your mind jumping uncontrollably from family to work to someone that annoys you?

Sure, we all have.

Using mindfulness, you can directly address this. Especially when you practice breath awareness. Breath awareness helps you control your own mind by helping you choose what you focus on.

Here's another example.

Have you ever experienced a dull mind where you find that it's hard to concentrate?

Most people have.

The problem with the dull mind is it makes you feel as if you have just woken up. Even worse, it can linger for the whole day.

Taking a few minutes to concentrate on your breathing can help snap you out of this disempowering state.

Of course, you've also experienced the agitated mind when your mind moves so fast that it seems uncontrollable. Mindfulness can help you focus on your breath so you can slow down and have a clearer mind.

The result of becoming mindful of your body or breath is that your thoughts and emotions become more balanced. This helps to clear and balance your mind.

Habits are groves your mind has made to help you do things without thinking too much about them. If that groove is to press the breaks when you come to a stop sign, that's a good thing.

But sometimes these unconscious grooves can cause you to react without thinking. This can lead to work and relationship problems.

Practicing mindfulness makes you aware of these slippery pathways. This awareness gives you the ability to change them. It does this by giving you a chance to reflect on the effectiveness of your responses like a scientist would, as an observer.

This new perspective can help you find a different option that will work better.

**Well-Being benefits of mindfulness**

As you regularly practice mindfulness, you will see quite a few improvements in your life. For example, you will experience a more peaceful mind.

Mindfulness also helps to bring moments of clarity, which can make you feel much more alive and connected.

Since it reduces the flow of mindless mental chatter, you will have more energy. You'll also feel better about yourself.

You can use a body scan meditation to observe your whole body's sensations. Some people that use this procedure find that they can experience their body for the first time, which helps them enjoy a richer experience of their emotional life.

Mindfulness also helps individuals in exploring deeper the existential questions like "what is my life's purpose?", "who am I?", and even "what's death?"

It is this deep, personal exploration of life that led to the development of mindfulness by its ancient practitioners.

Hopefully, this chapter has convinced you that the practice of mindfulness is an excellent investment.

But before we move on, let's discuss the importance of living in the present moment.

# Chapter 15

# The Importance of Living in the Present Moment

*"Few of us ever live in the present. We are forever anticipating what is to come or remembering what has gone."* - **Louis L'Amour**

IT'S HARD TO LIVE in the present. We think about past issues that still haunt us and imagine things that can go wrong in the future. This type of thinking can stress us out and make our lives miserable.

Living your life in the present is one of the best ways to reduce the stress that is brought from thoughts about what might come or have already gone by.

Living in the present means not worrying about what happened in the past. It removes the fear of what lies in the future.

It's all about enjoying life today.

But when you choose to live in the past or try to predict the future, it robs you of your enjoyment today. You can't live an authentic life.

This is how mindfulness helps. It helps you learn to live more in the present.

When you live in the present moment, negative thoughts will lose their power over you. This is the essence of mindfulness, to stay in the present as much as possible.

You do this by observing sensations non-judgmentally.

Practicing mindfulness in this way allows you to see your thoughts and emotions for what they are, simply thoughts and emotions you are having at this moment.

It also allows you to see much of life around you with fresh eyes.

Thoughts like "I am lonely", "No one loves me" or "I must be stupid" are often subtle but affect you, anyway. Your subconscious mind believes them uncritically.

They can affect you even more if you are feeling down because of events in your life.

But by simply allowing your thoughts to be, paying them no special attention, and not judging them, you can reduce their power over you. By being mindful and present, you starve them of the oxygen they need to live in your mind.

As a result, you realize they are just thoughts that you are having. You don't need to believe in them uncritically.

Emotions no longer affect you as strongly. You gain an understanding that feelings like anger, or any other potent emotions, are simply feelings and nothing more.

As you become more aware of your behavior patterns and thoughts, you're more likely to see a difficult situation as it takes form. This gives you a better chance of dealing with the situation in a more favorable way.

This awareness gives you more options.

Of course, you may choose to continue down your habitual path to deal with the situation. But even if you continue along the habitual path, your awareness allows you to choose constructive responses instead of reactive ones.

Living in the present moment also helps to slow down the chatter of your negative thoughts. This allows you to achieve a deeper sense of peace.

## Length of Practice

Mindfulness takes time and energy and, therefore, needs a great deal of commitment. Once you have started your practice, it's a good idea to set aside a certain length of time each day.

At first, this can just be a practice of five or ten minutes. Over time, aim for between 20 and 40 minutes, once or twice a day.

When teaching children to meditate, shorter periods of time of between 2 and 5 minutes may be helpful.

Next, let's see how you can incorporate mindfulness into your daily life.

# Chapter 16

# Mini Mindfulness Practice in Daily Life

*"As we encounter new experiences with a mindful and wise attention, we discover that one of three things will happen to our new experience: it will go away, it will stay the same, or it will get more intense. whatever happens does not really matter."* - **Jack Kornfield**

MINDFULNESS PRACTICE CAN BE a wonderful way to incorporate more peace and serenity into your daily life. Yet, with our busy schedules, it can be difficult to find the time to truly focus on mindful awareness.

But you don't need hours and hours of meditation. Just a few minutes a day can make a big difference.

You can practice mindfulness in everyday life by choosing to be mindful of one or two regular activities in your day.

Good examples are tooth brushing and dish washing. You can combine these with some mini-mindful exercises, and you will be good to go.

**Tooth Brushing**

Tooth brushing is something that you are probably (hopefully) doing every day, maybe once or twice.

As you brush your teeth you are most likely doing it in automatic mode as your mind wanders to some other activities of the past or the future.

But this is a great opportunity to practice mindfulness.

Pay attention to the toothbrush in your hand, the feel of the brush against each individual tooth, the taste of the paste, and any accompanying sounds.

Done this way, the whole tooth-brushing process can give you a 2 – 3-minute mindfulness session.

You can even include this activity in your to-do list to ensure you don't miss out on this exercise.

**Dish Washing**

Many people think dish washing is unpleasant.

But if you reframe it as an exercise for your mindfulness practice, it can become quite interesting.

Take your time as you wash each dish.

Be aware of each dish, each movement of your hand, the water, and the sound.

# Mini Mindfulness

Mini-mindfulness exercises can help you maintain mindfulness throughout the day.

This is composed of short regular mindfulness exercises done a few times during your day.

Here are a few simple tips for incorporating mini-mindfulness exercises into your everyday routine:

**Morning Breathing**

In the morning, take a few deep breaths in through your nose and out through your mouth. Concentrate on feeling the breath as it moves through your body. Doing this for just one minute can help you start your day in a calm and centered way.

**Focus on Lunch**

During your lunch break, try to eat without distractions such as phone, laptop, or the TV. Eating mindfully will help you savor and appreciate each bite and will also make it easier to digest your food properly.

**Notice the World Around You**

When commuting home, try to really notice the environment around you. Instead of zoning out and getting lost in thoughts about work or chores that need to be done, focus on the sights, smells, and sounds of the journey.

By taking small steps like these every day, you can start to cultivate more mindfulness and presence in your life, no matter how busy your day is!

You can use your daily practice to train your mind to deal with distractions and shift into a mindful state.

This is what we're going to work on next.

# Chapter 17

# A Life filled With Distractions

*"Mindfulness isn't difficult, we just need to remember to do it."* - **Sharon Salzberg**

YOU ALREADY KNOW THAT our modern lifestyles bring a lot of distractions. This can make it hard to concentrate.

Information bombards us faster, louder, and more in your face than ever before. We can't open our computers or devices without being assailed by social media, marketing, and entertainment, all vying for our attention.

This pulls our minds away from more important work.

What's worse, as these things shift our attention, they condition us to respond to their stimulus, like lab rats. Being plugged in all the time has changed the way we live, and not for the better.

It can make us constantly distracted.

This is where practicing mindfulness can help.

## Mindfully Dealing with Distractions

Unless you completely unplug, you can't block out all these distractions. And even if you get rid of these distractions, there will always be others.

But this isn't what mindfulness does. Practicing mindfulness isn't trying to block out other things, but about noticing them. Once you notice them and determine that your attention does not need to be there, you can bring your attention back to where it needs to be.

You can't force yourself to block things out. If you try, you make things more apparent.

Right now, don't think of a pink elephant. Whatever you do, don't think of a pink elephant.

What are you thinking of right now?

An irritating pink elephant!

Instead of ignoring, practicing mindfulness involves noticing things and acknowledging that they are there, but then deciding they may not be important.

This is especially important with destructive emotions. You want to notice them and acknowledge that they exist. You then allow yourself to feel how they are affecting you, without fighting against them.

You just allow them to be and let them pass.

This is what this next exercise will help you do.

Right now, sit comfortably. As I guide you through this exercise, really focus on each of the senses. Except for the seeing part of the exercise, you can close your eyes if it helps you focus.

First, notice five things you can see.

Look around the room and notice five things you would not normally see. For example, a piece of furniture, the flooring, a crack in the ceiling, etc.

Next, notice four things you can feel with your hands or skin. This could be the texture of your clothes, the cool air on your skin, the hardness of the floor beneath your bottom, etc.

In this third part of the exercise, notice three things you can hear. Maybe background noises, like a car outside, a bird singing, an airplane flying overhead, etc.

Now notice two things you can smell. These can be pleasant or unpleasant odors. Perhaps the smell of food cooking, the floor you're sitting on, a fragrance, etc.

Finally, notice one thing you can taste. You can bite a piece of food or cookie or piece of candy. You can take a sip of something to drink, tea, coffee or even water. Just taste whatever is now in your mouth.

This exercise helps bring you into a mindfulness state quickly. It does this by helping you focus on the present moment, by being more aware of what surrounds you.

Being able to focus on the present helps you focus on 'what is' rather than on 'what if'. If you worry about things that might or might not happen, you are worrying about things that are not real.

Instead, you can use this exercise to focus on the present to stop this needless worry.

This doesn't mean to stop planning. You still need to plan. Mindful planning differs from worrying about what might happen in the future.

Worrying about things that might happen can make you feel overwhelmed and stressed. Focusing on 'what is' helps you make plans with a rational mind.

You are aware of potential threats and opportunities. This helps you to plan. Planning this way helps you feel calm and in control.

Learning from the past differs from reliving the past and regretting what happened.

Remembering the past and learning from it is constructive. Reliving the past and worrying about what transpired will only make you feel stressed.

Ruminating this way only evokes unpleasant emotions from memories that you can't do anything about.

By learning to deal with distractions, you can live in the only time you have to do anything, the present.

Now that you have a method you can use to deal with distractions, let's see how you can quickly learn to incorporate mindfulness into your life.

# Chapter 18

# Tips for Rapid Improvement

*"Patience is a form of wisdom. It demonstrates that we understand and accept the fact that sometimes things must unfold in their own time."* —— **Jon Kabat-Zinn**

THERE IS A STORY about a young, beginning martial artist who wanted badly to advance in his studies so he could earn his black belt. Since this was his goal, he went to ask his teacher for his advice.

After the young student bowed politely, the instructor queried, "How may I help you?"

Taking in and then letting out a deep breath, the young student responded, "I want to earn my black belt. How long will it take me if I come five days a week?"

Smiling, the teacher replied, "Five years."

The young student looked at the floor, and then back at his teacher and asked, "What if I came to every class and practiced every day at home, how long would it take?"

Still smiling, the teacher told him, "Ten years."

The student's face dropped. Then he said, "What if I practiced night and day, every day, only stopping to eat and sleep? How long would it take then?"

The teacher's eyes twinkled as he replied, "Twenty years."

Sputtering, the young student nearly shouted, "Why is it every time I say I will work harder, you tell me it will take longer?"

Taking a slow breath, the teacher smiled and said, "When you have one eye focused on the goal, you only have one eye to focus on the path."

Continuing, the teacher said, "The only way you will ever become a black belt is to be patient and enjoy the journey. Then your goal will only be another step along your path."

## The Need for Patience

Whether it's practicing martial arts, mindfulness by meditating or using visualization, when people start, they often get discouraged and give up.

Why is this?

One problem is that too many of us, like the young student, want to get immediate results. We expect to feel different instantly.

When this doesn't happen, we end up frustrated and stressed. This is an unhelpful attitude, especially when learning mindfulness meditation.

Like going to the martial arts gym, mindfulness meditation is an exercise for the mind. Just as it takes time to strengthen your body, it's going to take time to strengthen your mind.

This means nudging your mind in the direction you want it to go instead of forcing it. Let your mind do whatever it wants.

When you try forcing it in one or another direction, you lose that all-important freedom. Now, instead of relaxing, you're producing stress hormones.

Be tolerant and have patience. Try not to get upset with yourself if your mind keeps wandering or you keep getting distracted. It's normal.

If your face gets itchy, scratch it. If you're thirsty, get up and get a glass of water.

Don't try to force anything, just let yourself 'be' as you are.

If you really want help jump-starting your progress, consider 'priming' yourself. Priming is a term used in psychology that simply refers to preparing your brain in a certain way.

Sometimes this means influencing your mental state by giving yourself a certain stimulus. This might be a photo of a field of flowers or a warm sunny day at a park.

In other cases, it means changing your emotions. In this case, doing something calming that also requires you to focus just before you try meditating.

For example, you might try relaxing in a beautiful but novel location. New scenery increases neurotransmitters and hormones associated with focus. At the same time, being in a natural environment helps make you more relaxed. It also encourages slower brainwaves.

Finally, like the young martial arts student, don't be too ambitious regarding how often you intend to practice. This is another classic mistake, setting the idea that you're going to make a practice of meditating for 30 minutes every day from the very beginning.

Unless you're already extremely disciplined, this intention, while admirable, is destined for failure. Build your discipline by starting with something small. Even just 5 minutes right as you wake up will work.

Over time, you can build on this habit.

This is what the teacher was trying to help his student understand. Small habits, built slowly and mindfully, will make a big difference in your life.

Now, let's look at how to relax.

# Chapter 19

# Dealing with Problems and Distractions

*"If you feel lost, disappointed, hesitant, or weak, return to yourself, to who you are, here and now and when you get there, you will discover yourself, like a lotus flower in full bloom, even in a muddy pond, beautiful and strong. "*- **Masaru Emoto**

IN MINDFULNESS MEDITATION, DISTRACTIONS and frustrations are an unavoidable part of the practice.

This can often leave you feeling annoyed and discouraged, like you're failing. But it's important to keep in mind that these feelings are normal and are a valuable part of the learning process.

Rather than trying to push away these feelings or run from them, take some time to recognize and observe them. Simply noticing your frustrations can be enough to shift your mind patterns in a more positive direction.

When distractions or frustrations arise during your meditation, take a moment to acknowledge how you feel before gently returning your focus back to your breathing or meditation session.

With practice and patience, this process will become easier and eventually you can use distractions and frustration as opportunities for growth rather than seeing them as setbacks.

But you want to reduce external distractions, especially in the beginning, as much as possible.

Here's how:

- Unplug or switch off all your phones.
- Request those in your home to give you some quiet time, if possible.
- Turn off all computers, televisions, and anything electronic.

Every effort you make to reduce distractions will have a beneficial effect on your mindfulness practice.

But keep in mind that everyday events will always get into the way of your practice and there are ways to deal with them.

For example, if you become distracted by sounds, listen to them and let them form part of your practice rather than trying to block them out.

Here are some ways to manage internal distractions:

- Always be patient. It is natural for your mind to think, so to be fair to yourself, let it.
- If there's something urgent that you need to deal with, do it before you meditate. This will allow your mind to be more at rest during your meditation session.
- Welcome your thoughts and notice how they make you feel.

- You can visualize the stream of thoughts that arise in your mind like clouds that pass across the sky. Also, you can see the thoughts as separate from you and note what effect that separation has.

Meditation is about experiencing whatever is happening right now. Painful and blissful experiences come and go, so you need to just keep watching without holding on to either.

While meditating, you may sometimes experience flashing lights, floating, physical pain, flying pigs, sleepiness, boredom, or anything you can feel or that your mind can imagine. This is okay.

You may also suffer from perfectionism, striving to do everything as perfectly as possible. Let it go.

Whenever these feelings come up, remember they are just experiences, then try to return to focusing on meditating.

You don't need to analyze these experiences, but let them go as far as you can, then come back to your senses in the here and now.

Mindfulness meditation is patience training.

To connect with the senses or the breath requires you to be patient.

For example, if you recognize you are feeling impatient with your practice, but you continue to sit there, then you are training your patience muscle.

Being in a hurry to get results from your mindfulness practice can make you feel impatient. But the more you understand the benefits of this practice, the more you will also understand the wisdom of being patient.

This allows you to enjoy the full benefits.

The more impatient you are, the harder it will be for you to get the results you're looking for.

After deciding on how long you are going to practice mindfulness, stick to it.

You spend your life trying to get somewhere, achieving something, struggling, and putting in a lot of effort. Since you're already striving, let the benefits of mindfulness to be at the top of your list of things you're trying to achieve in life.

Meditation is a special time for you to let go of all outside activities and struggles and be in the moment.

In case you cannot cope with being still for 10 minutes while paying attention to your breath, reduce the time to 5 minutes, and if that is still too much, try even 2 minutes.

Even 10 seconds of mindfulness meditation is fine as a starting point.

Begin with as much time as you can manage, then build it up, a little at a time.

What matters is to keep at it and never to give up.

Practice as regularly as you can, slowly escalating the time you want to invest.

Now that you understand how to deal with distractions, let's move on to relaxation.

# Chapter 20

# A Beginner's Guide to Relaxation

*"Mindfulness is deliberately paying full attention to what is happening around you– in your body, heart, and mind. Mindfulness is awareness without criticism or judgment."* – **Jan Chozen Bays**

FOR MANY PEOPLE, RELAXATION means sitting down in front of a television at the end of a stressful day. However, this does not reduce the harmful effects that emotional distress has on us, both physically and mentally.

The best way to reduce emotional distress effectively is to activate your body's natural relaxation response.

A simple way to do this is by practicing relaxation techniques that you enjoy, such as meditation, breathing, mindfulness, visualization, yoga or rhythmic exercise.

**Learning to relax is a skill**

Like nearly everything in life, relaxation is a skill that you will have to learn.

You can start with a short relaxation session that lasts for about 5 minutes. As you gain more experience, you can extend your sessions for longer periods of time, up to 20 or 30 minutes, or even longer.

Set aside some time every day to relax, perhaps first thing in the morning or just before bedtime.

Initially, it is best to practice relaxation when you are feeling calm.

Also, try to find a place that is free of distractions.

**Finding the relaxation technique that works best for you**

There is no single relaxation technique that is best for everyone.

So, when choosing a relaxation technique that works best for you, consider things like your fitness level and the way you react to stress.

The best choice is one that feels comfortable to you and helps you to focus your mind in a manner that interrupts your everyday thoughts.

You also want it to fit into your lifestyle.

**Relaxation for different types of emotional distress**

How you are feeling influences the relaxation technique that works best for you.

For example, if you feel on edge, frustrated, angry, anxious, or stressed, the best relaxation techniques are ones that help you feel calm, such as visualization, deep breathing, or mindfulness.

When feeling lethargic, withdrawn, in a bad mood, or simply lacking energy, your best response is to use relaxation techniques that stimulate you. These could be swimming, walking, dancing, or anything rhythmic.

If you like to practice alone, then relaxation techniques such as progressive muscle relaxation or meditation will give you the space you need to have a peaceful mind and recharge.

Now, let's look at a simple relaxation technique that is also used in many types of mediation practices: belly breathing.

# Chapter 21

# Belly Breathing

*"Breath is the finest gift of nature. Be grateful for this wonderful gift."* - **Amit Ray**

ONE WAY TO DEVELOP mindfulness is to use one of life's basic processes, breathing, to focus your attention. By focusing on your breath, you can use the power of curiosity to rediscover how to mind your mind.

Deep breathing is an effective relaxation technique which is easy to learn. It is a technique I teach all my martial arts to calm themselves, especially when sparring.

For those of you that are unfamiliar with the term, sparring is when two people practice their martial arts skills against each other in a safe environment. Deep breathing allows them to keep their fight-or-flight response in check and is a quick way to reduce stress levels, almost anywhere.

Deep breathing is the foundation of many other relaxation practices. You simply need a few minutes and a place to sit comfortably, preferably with no distractions.

First, let's glance at the two types of breathing.

## Diaphragmatic breathing

Diaphragmatic breathing is how babies breathe. It's also how you breathe while sleeping.

This type of breathing uses your diaphragm to bring air deep into your lungs. When the diaphragm contracts, it descends, making room for your lungs to expand and air to fill them.

If you are breathing with your diaphragm, your stomach will rise and fall with your breaths.

## Costal breathing

Costal breathing works by opening and closing the rib area. Using this type of breathing, you are only breathing into the upper part of your lungs.

When you breathe costally, you leave over fifty percent of your lungs uninflated and without air.

Another problem with costal breathing is if you breathe like this in a highly stressful event, such as sparring, your lungs wil rapidly run out of air. This will deplete your body of the fuel it needs to continue to operate, oxygen.

If you continue to breathe like this, it can cause you to hyperventilate or pass out. This isn't an outcome anyone desires.

## Practicing belly breathing

This technique requires you to breathe deeply into your tummy and get as much fresh air as possible in your lungs.

**Procedure**
- Sit at a comfortable place with your back straight.
- Put one hand on your stomach and the other on your chest, then notice your breathing.
- Breathe slowly and gently, transfer most of your breathing to your tummy so you can feel that the movement occurring there.
- The muscles of your stomach should rise and fall as you breathe.
- It can help to count as you breathe.
- Breathe in for three counts and out for four counts, maintaining a comfortable and steady rhythm and try to avoid holding your breath in between each count.
- Try to inhale enough so that your lower abdomen rises and falls.
- For this technique to become beneficial to you, it is helpful to practice it regularly, maybe twice a day, for a few minutes at a time.
- Return to normal breathing if you feel dizzy.

As you think about deep breathing meditation practice, did you get distracted while trying to concentrate on breathing?

What was distracting you?

There are many internal and external distractions that can redirect your attention. External distractions can be things we see, noises like cell phones or social media pings.

Internal distractions can be thoughts that suddenly appear, such as, 'What am I going to eat for lunch', or 'I don't think I have enough time to finish this project'.

While they aren't always negative, distractions can become bad when they make us feel stressed.

For example, if we feel overwhelmed by too many demands on our attention. Or if we ruminate or dwell on negative thoughts, on things that are not even real but imaginary dangers.

You can use mindfulness to help control your thoughts and take back control of your thinking. A little later, you'll do an exercise that will help you deal with distractions.

For now, practice deep breathing as often as possible. The great thing about belly breathing is you can practice it anywhere.

Practice in the car, in the line at the store, at a meeting, and anywhere else you can think of. Like all skills, the more you practice belly breathing, the better you'll become.

Next, let's see how to enhance your mindfulness practice.

# Chapter 22

# Practicing Mindfulness

> *"Mindfulness gives you time. Time gives you choices. Choices, skillfully made, lead to freedom. You don't have to be swept away by your feelings. You can respond with wisdom and kindness rather than habit and reactivity."* –**Bhante Henepola Gunaratana**

YOU CAN PRACTICE MANY mindfulness exercises anywhere and anytime. People practice mindfulness while walking or washing dishes.

When you practice more structured mindfulness exercises, such as body scan meditation or sitting meditation, set aside time to be in a quiet place where you can sit without distractions or interruptions. These exercises are better practiced early in the morning before you begin your daily routine or later in the evening before going to bed.

We'll look more deeply at these a little later in this book.

First, let's go through some basics.

## Preparation

To get the most from your practice, you need to prepare. The following are guidelines you can use to prepare yourself for mindfulness meditation.

### Choosing a place to meditate

Select a place where you feel comfortable meditating. This place should not be too dark or too bright and should also not be too hot or too cold.

Try to avoid places that can have distractions and disturbances.

### Decide on a suitable posture

There are many postures that you can choose from–sitting, standing, walking, or lying down. Choose and test different ones to figure out the kind that suits you best.

## Practicing Meditation

Once you have chosen the posture that works best for you, relax in that position. Settle into your meditation and then examine the four foundations of mindfulness.

These foundations are:

1. **Mindfulness of the body**

This involves focusing, mentally noting, and exploring parts of the body such as teeth, hair, skin, head, stomach, bones, muscles, etc.

**2. Mindfulness of physical sensations and feelings**

Focus on how and when sensations occur. Are they unpleasant, pleasant, or neutral? Study how the mind and body interact with these feelings.

The skills you get here will teach you tolerance of the body.

**3. The mindfulness of mental states**

This will include your ideas, thoughts, images, dreams, etc. Watch how they come up and change and how they arise dependent on outside impulses or feelings or the amount of concentration you have.

You can also decide to let go of these mental experiences.

**4. Mindfulness of the consciousness**

Here you will find states of mind such as a focused mind or mind that are unfocused, tiredness or energetic states, etc.

Is your mind dominated by some feelings such as anger or greed?

These types of questions create awareness of your current state of mind.

**Take Note**

When you are focusing, you can note things mentally or verbally.

Noting a thing mentally is the best since it builds concentration, but if it is easier for you to note things verbally, do it that way. Taking note can help you see how the mind reacts to knowledge and words.

But you have to be wary not to get absorbed in a story. Strive to work towards silent awareness and eventually to word-less awareness.

**Let Go**

Let go of any stressful states in your mind and body that may come up.

Be kind to yourself and try to avoid judging yourself.

If your mind jumps to bewilderment, fear, confusion, distress, or condemnation, it means your mind is still learning how to stay mindful.

This simply means you'll need to practice more to cultivate a peaceful mind. In fact, to maintain that peaceful mind, you'll need to continue practicing for the rest of your life.

Now, let's look at how you can incorporate mindfulness into your daily life.

# Chapter 23

# Mindfulness in Daily Life

WHEN I FIRST BEGAN practicing mindfulness, I thought it would be like my meditation practice, which was formal. As I meditated, I sat in a place set aside specifically in my apartment for meditation and practiced at the same time every day.

Practicing mindfulness is different. The great thing about mindfulness is you can practice it anywhere. There are no special times for practicing. You can practice anytime you decide to tune yourself into the present moment.

For example, right now, feel your legs and butt pressing on the chair you're sitting on.

Take a moment right now to reflect on this.

How comfortable are you right now?

Does any part of your body hurt?

Can you feel your clothes against your body?

How warm are you?

Are you leaning more on the right or the left?

Here, you can use mindfulness to fix your posture. But you can also use it to improve your abilities in sports or just move your body more efficiently.

Simply by practicing mindfulness exercises based on sensations and by becoming more aware of what is going on around you, you can spend more time in the present. This is useful because very often you'll find that your mind isn't where it should be.

For example, maybe you're walking through a beautiful scenic park, but you are thinking about work. Then, as far as your body is concerned, you may as well be at work.

You can use mindfulness to make yourself more aware of where you are and to pay attention to what's around you. This means feeling the breeze on your skin, looking at the beautiful flowers and smelling the clear air.

Mindfully walking through the park allows you to benefit more from the experience. As you slow down and notice the flowers, trees, and sunshine, you appreciate being able to be part of the world around you.

Practicing mindfulness also can help you become calmer and, simultaneously, more productive. The ability to stay calm is essential to staying focused, and your focus allows you to get more done.

Changing your communication style can alter the way people perceive you.

For example, you might listen more mindfully and then restate your understanding to ensure you're both on the same page. This allows you to communicate more clearly with fewer misunderstandings.

You'll also be able to identify negative emotions as temporary and destructive, reducing their effect on you.

For example, you can simply notice that you're getting angry. As you notice, you'll be aware that feeling angry contaminates your thinking. This awareness allows you to take the steps necessary to deal with your anger before it gets out of hand.

With practice, you can become more aware of people and things that trigger you. This can help reduce the stress and anxiety you experience from them.

As your habitual repetitive anxious thinking fades away, you'll find that you have more time for more important activities like problem solving, creativity, appreciating music, or developing deep relationships.

It is just as simple as that.

Mindfulness can help you leave your problems behind, making it easier for you to find happiness in everyday life.

As you learn to observe your sensations and live in the present, nearly all your problems will evaporate into thin air. You'll feel as light and free as a child at play.

One other important aspect of mindfulness is remembering.

Here, we're not referring to remembering as memories of past events. Instead, we're talking about remembering to pay attention and being aware.

Most of the time, we don't know what we're focused on or what we're paying attention to. We regularly try to do more than one thing at a time.

When we do more than one thing at a time, or multitask, we do some tasks on autopilot. Our brains run many tasks in the background without us consciously perceiving them.

For example, when someone is practicing martial arts, they do a lot of things at the same time. Let's say they are practicing their forms, which are hand and foot movements done in a pre-determined pattern. This is like ballet or other dances, only with kicking and punching.

When they are first learning their form, they pay close attention to the movements of their hands and feet. In the beginning, their instructor will give them lots of feedback to help them improve.

But after many practice sessions, they can go through the form subconsciously. They do it flawlessly and without consciously thinking about what they are doing.

This is the same for many things we do. Think back to the first time you drove a car. When you got into the car, you adjusted the seat, the side mirrors, and the rear-view mirror.

Your hands were at the two and ten position on the steering wheel. You swiveled your head to look for cars and pedestrians. You paid attention to the pressure you were putting on the accelerator and break.

You were intentionally and consciously thinking about your driving.

Fast forward to today. You jump in the car and go. While you probably still do everything you did before, but you are doing it subconsciously.

You're doing these tasks automatically, without effort.

Over time, we consign many tasks to our subconscious muscle memory, and this is a good thing. It allows us to use our brains more efficiently.

What would your life be like if you had to think about how to tie your shoes every morning? How about if you had to pay attention to walking while talking? Breathing and reading?

I think you can see what I'm getting at. Our brain's ability to multitask is what allows us to walk down the stairs, eat and read, walk and talk.

It also allows us to take in external stimuli like smells, sounds, and lights, as well as internal ones like hunger, muscle tightness etc. and unconsciously turn them into actionable information. This allows us to move easily through the world instead of spending our time and brainpower thinking about how and where to put our feet on the ground to walk.

While this is good for walking, it's not so good for remembering to pay attention. These habitual patterns can impede our ability to pay the conscious attention needed for higher cognition tasks, like listening to your child or significant other, writing an important email or class paper, or developing a business plan.

This is because we can only do these types of tasks well, one at a time. As a result, we forget things, adopt bad habits, and stress out when we should enjoy what life brings.

But as you continue practicing mindfulness, you'll find you're better able to regulate your thoughts. This allows you to decide what you want to improve and how you want to improve it.

This is the importance of intention. Intentional thinking will be at the very core of your mindfulness practice.

## Chapter 24

# Mindful Focus - One Step at a Time

"You have a treasure within you that is infinitely greater than anything the world can offer." - **Eckhart Tolle**

IT'S VERY POSSIBLE TO feel overwhelmed and intimidated when faced with large goals. Because mindfulness practice trains us to focus on the moment, it can help reduce these feelings by focusing your mind on doing one small step at a time.

Imagine your goal is to climb up a gigantic mountain, like Mount Everest. If you look up at the entire mountain, it's likely you'll feel overwhelmed. This can lead to being discouraged and thinking about giving up.

Mountaineers instead focus on specific areas to climb to. If you're climbing Mount Everest from the South side, your first stop after the airport would be the 17,300 foot South Side Base Camp. Here you would acclimatize for a few days.

Then you would climb through the Khumbu icefall, up the Western Cwm, which is Welsh for "valley".

Next you would climb up to the Lhotse Face and on to the South Col, which is the lowest point of a ridge or saddle between two peaks, in this case Mount Everest and Lhotse, the highest and fourth-highest mountains in the world.

Finally, you'll climb up to the South Summit, the Hillary Step and on to the Summit at 29,035 feet.

While you'll need to reach these milestones, you'll also have smaller goals along the way. You'll focus on the next boulder and then, the next turn in the trail and around a crevice and so on.

But, step-by-step, eventually you will have climbed the whole mountain.

This is how mindfulness can help. It trains you to focus on the one thing you're doing right now. By focusing on one task at a time, eventually you will complete the mountainous goal you have set for yourself.

This is the same for any gigantic task you face, like writing a book or graduating from college. It gets done one word at a time or one class at a time.

## Putting Things Off

What happens when you keep putting off a task that you know you're supposed to do?

How did you feel?

Maybe not so good, right?

Why are you putting off the task?

It might be because you're not focusing on the next step, but being overwhelmed by the enormity of your goal.

When this happens, don't beat yourself up. Just notice what you are feeling. Allow yourself to feel this way for a moment and then mindfully bring your attention back to the next task you need to complete.

Here's a mindfulness exercise to help you train your mind to do this.

Sit in a comfortable position.

Allow your eyes to close.

Now, imagine that your ability to hear is like a radio that you can use to dial into different channels.

The first channel has the sounds of the room. As you tune into this channel, what can you hear?

You're still aware of sounds coming from inside the room, but don't pay any attention to them.

Now, change the channel and tune into the sounds inside the room.

What are you hearing?

Pay attention to the sounds inside the room.

Again, change the channel.

This channel is tuned into the sounds inside your body.

As you tune into the sounds inside your body, perform a body scan.

Focus on any sounds you can hear, your breathing, your heartbeat, any sound within your body.

Tune into each part of your body, starting from your toes, your legs to the top of your head.

Now, change the channel again.

Tune into your breathing only.

Listen to the sounds in the room.

Switch the channel again and listen to the sounds furthest away.

Listen outside of the room. As far away as you can hear.

Now, one last time, come back to your breathing.

When you are ready, allow your eyes to open.

How do you feel after you went through this exercise?

What were the hardest and the easiest things to do?

This exercise helps you train your mind to move its attention mindfully between different stimuli.

Here, it's auditory stimuli.

You probably found that while you were listening to one channel, sounds from the other channels would pop up.

The purpose of the exercise was to ignore them gently, without forcing yourself to block them out.

You want to train your mind to only focus on what you want it to focus on while still being aware of everything that's going on.

This is where mindfulness can help, giving you the ability to be aware of everything but choosing to concentrate on the task at hand.

This also allows you to switch your attention between one task and another, as you discovered in this exercise.

You can take this practice into your everyday life. If you are writing a proposal and the phone rings, stop writing, pick up the phone and focus on the call.

When the call is over, start writing again.

This allows you to switch tasks according to their priorities.

Now, instead of trying to multitask, you can focus your attention on one thing at a time.

The key is to focus enough on each task, so you do not switch your attention too quickly or as a continuous stream of events.

This is just rapid single-tasking, which is almost the same as multi-tasking and can lead to poor performance and stress.

As you mindfully train your attention to focus on a task, you improve your ability to plan and organize tasks.

One task at a time is all you can do, so use mindfulness to help you focus on that one thing.

Next, let's look at how we can use mindfulness in therapeutic settings.

# Chapter 25

# Therapeutic Mindfulness

*"If you want to conquer the anxiety of life, live in the moment, live in the breath."* —— **Amit Ray**

THE REASON BUDDHIST PRACTITIONERS train mindfulness is to attain the omniscient transcendental wisdom, not only in formal meditation, but in daily activities such as walking, sitting, eating, and working. These formal practitioners used mindfulness to find wisdom.

Fast forward to the modern use of mindfulness, where Western psychotherapy has adopted mindfulness for therapeutic purposes.

When Jon Kabat-Zinn brought mindfulness to the West in the 1970s, he provided mindfulness training as a method for stress reduction. He later founded the Center for Mindfulness at the

University of Massachusetts Medical School, that uses mindfulness therapeutically.

Mindfulness is now used in many institutions, such as medical, wellness, and sports. Lately, schools have adopted mindfulness practice to help calm young students while improving their focus and grades.

Yoga and Tai Chi are also methods of practicing mindfulness. I was first introduced to mindfulness while practicing Tai chi. They also practiced it in the yoga classes I took later.

One result of this is the definition of mindfulness has expanded. It now includes qualities such as compassion, acceptance, and non-judgment, which are all part of Jon Kabat-Zinn's therapeutic mindfulness.

Here's a definition of therapeutic mindfulness. "The awareness that emerges through paying attention on purpose, in the present moment and non-judgmentally to the unfolding of experience moment to moment."

A simpler definition of therapeutic mindfulness is being aware of your present experience and accepting it for what it is.

It is concerned with the adoption of a particular orientation toward an individual's experience that is characterized by openness, acceptance, and curiosity.

Therapeutic mindfulness is used to treat a variety of different mental and physical medical conditions. By focusing one's attention on the present, it can help to address life concerns.

Some examples of the health and life benefits of therapeutic mindfulness include improving memory and focus.

In the last chapter, we discussed the issues while trying to pay attention to more than one high cognitive task, or thinking task, at the same time. For example, writing emails while talking to somebody on the phone, while trying to remember what's needed for the meeting at two o'clock.

Trying to do all this simultaneously can make us feel overwhelmed and anxious. This anxiety can lead to Attention Deficit Trait (ADT) which differs from Attention Deficit Disorder (ADD).

While ADD is a psychological disorder, which is a combination of environmental and psychological factors, ADT is purely environmental. It results from being constantly bombarded with too much information.

It's this informational assault that impairs your critical thinking. Intentionally deciding what to focus on helps decrease your stress and anxiety.

This can lead to improved relationships and help you resolve inner experiences, increasing your overall life satisfaction.

We'll return to this a little later. Right now, let's explore how mindfulness fits in with social psychology.

# Chapter 26

# Mindfulness and Social Psychology

*"As we encounter new experiences with a mindful and wise attention, we discover that one of three things will happen to our new experience: it will go away, it will stay the same, or it will get more intense. whatever happens does not really matter."* - **Jack Kornfield**

MINDFULNESS AND SOCIAL PSYCHOLOGY go hand in hand.

Social psychology is the study of how the presence or behavior of other people influences an individual's or group's behavior. Its focus is to answer how and why people's perceptions and actions are influenced by environmental factors.

For example, you act and think differently among people you know than you do among strangers. Do you wonder why that is?

Social psychologists spend their careers trying to determine the answers to these questions and others like them. Using laboratory-based findings, researchers conduct empirical studies to answer specific questions.

Here are some examples:

Is a person's behavior an accurate indication of their personality?

Is social behavior goal oriented?

Does social perception influence behavior? In what ways?

How do we form destructive social attitudes, like prejudice?

Social psychology is therefore concerned with the way these thoughts, feelings, intentions and goals are constructed and, in turn, how these factors influence our interactions with other people. To help them better interpret these studies, social psychologists also use intrapersonal phenomena and interpersonal phenomena.

Social psychologists agree that reality is much too complex to easily make sense of. This means that humans tend to see the world as simplified images or schemas of reality.

A schema is simply a mental representation that allows a person to organize their knowledge in such a way that they feel that they know what to expect from a situation and experience. Schemas are developed based on information a person has gathered in their life experiences and then stored in memory.

Your brain creates and uses schemas as a short cut to make future encounters with similar situations easier to navigate. Some of the different types of schemas are discussed below.

## Roles

Role schemas help people to understand the social context with which they are engaged. This allows them to adjust accordingly to the demands of the situation.

For example, if you are employed as a physician, you will (hopefully) display your professional role in a hospital. But when you are with your family on a vacation you will most likely behave differently.

This implies that an observer will expect to see you behave differently depending on the social situation you are experiencing.

## Person

Apart from developing expectations about other people based on their social roles, we also develop expectations about their behavior based on their personality traits.

For example, when someone is quiet and shy in nature, then that is how the people who know them expect them to behave no matter where they are. On the other hand, if someone is open and outgoing and acted quiet and shy, we would infer that there might be something going on in this person's life or that the situation makes them feel uncomfortable.

## Self

Just like we expect others to behave in a particular way in certain situations, we also have expectations about how we should act in certain situations.

For example, if you believe that you are outgoing and people like talking to you at gatherings, then you will feel obligated to modify your behavior to fit this schema.

## Events

There are schemas for specific events which are referred to as scripts. These are based on expectations of how to behave in a variety of situations. They are also based on our associations with how events should play out based on our previous experiences with similar events.

We'll visit some of these a little later. Right now, let's explore how you can use mindfulness.

# Chapter 27

# How to Use Mindfulness

> *"Mindfulness isn't difficult. We just need to remember to do it."* –**Sharon Salzberg**

SINCE I HAD PRACTICED meditation before being introduced to mindfulness, I really wasn't sure how to begin. Maybe you aren't sure what to do either. This is what this chapter is all about, introducing you to how you can use mindfulness.

But, before we continue, let's do another exercise. In this exercise, you're going to cultivate self-compassion.

Write a few things you love about yourself. Don't worry if they sound self-serving or vain. Just acknowledge the things you like about yourself without judging.

Now mindfully do this exercise!

How do you feel after giving yourself some love?

Two key concepts of mindfulness are self-compassion and acceptance of self and others. In the default mode that we talked about earlier, we often beat ourselves up. We pay attention to the things that went wrong, or things we failed to achieve.

Self-compassion is about accepting our limits as human beings. This doesn't mean making excuses when we come up short, but learning from our mistakes and using the knowledge we get from them to become better.

As we become more compassionate towards ourselves, we also become more accepting of others as well.

The problem of being negative and overcritical is this can become a habitual way of looking at the world. As this mindset becomes a habit, we get better at being critical. The more we do this, the better we get at it. We reinforce our negative mindset, and it becomes a never-ending circle of gloom.

Using mindfulness to focus on compassion and positivity, you practice the skills of compassion and acceptance and reinforce these traits instead. This is how you can change the cycle of negativity.

Now that you've given yourself some love, let's check out some ways you can use mindfulness, beginning today.

## Guided Meditation

One of the simplest ways to start your mindfulness practice is using guided meditations. Guided meditations are simply recordings or videos that instruct you on what to do as you try meditating.

You can find many of these online. YouTube is a good starting point for your search.

The recording might begin by telling you to close your eyes and breathe in and out through the nose. Then they might tell you to think about your body or do a body scan.

Excellent tools for this are Headspace and Muse. You can download both apps for Android and iOS. Headspace is also available to use through the web. You'll require a headset with Muse.

Both apps have a few free guided meditations you can get started with. There are other apps you can choose from as well.

Most guided mindfulness meditations will walk you through a very similar process. Once you learn the steps, you can go through them on your own, without someone talking you through them.

To help you learn these steps, let's review them now.

**Step 1: Control Your Breathing**

The first thing to do is to breathe. An easy way to do this is to adopt the 'equal breathing' process from yoga.

In this practice, you breathe in through your nose and out through your mouth. Hold each inhalation and exhalation for around 3 seconds ('equal' breathing). As you inhale, you fill your lungs with fresh oxygen. You expel all the $CO_2$ with your exhalation.

Of course, you can use any kind of breathing so long as it is slow, deliberate, and full. On the Headspace App they advise you to 'breathe loud enough so that the person next to you could hear you'.

Why all this emphasis on breathing?

We humans breathe rapidly when stressed. It's part of the 'fight or flight' response. This rapid breathing allows us to get more oxygen and energy into our bodies quickly.

When you breathe slowly and deeply, you're letting your body know that you're safe. This helps you exit the 'fight or flight' state and enter the 'rest and digest' state.

In this state, your heart rate slows, your cortisol levels fall, and you become more relaxed.

We'll cover deep breathing again later.

**Step 2: Pay Attention to Your Senses**

In the next step, you are often told to focus on your physical senses. This means noticing the smells, sounds and even the temperature of the room.

When you are practicing guided meditation, your eyes are normally closed, so you won't be using sight.

You're not 'looking' for sounds or straining to hear them. Instead, you are simply paying attention to the sounds that you don't normally listen to.

You might find that you can hear creaking in the house. Maybe you can hear your neighbors. If it's raining, perhaps you can hear the wind and rain. On a nice day, you probably hear birds.

This is a reminder of just how little we normally pay attention to our senses. It also is an example of how much richer our experience becomes as we practice mindfulness.

**Step 3: Body Scan**

While you can use body scan meditation on its own, you can use it as part of any meditation session. The idea is simply to become more aware of your own body.

You do this by systematically starting at the top of the head and then moving gradually through your body down to the toes. As you scan your body, you notice how you feel.

You can use this process to help you sleep. The best way to do this is using muscle relaxation, which is first tensing and then releasing each part of your body as you move through it.

What you'll find is that you carry large amounts of tension everywhere in your body, from the muscles in your face, to your neck, to your arms and legs. As you feel tension, you acknowledge it let it go.

This will help you feel far more relaxed. Eventually, this will enable you to fall into a deep and restful sleep.

Right now, though, you're just scanning your body and using this process to become more mindful of how it feels. This will help you begin the process of introspection and self-directed attention.

**Step 4: Focus on Breathing**

After noticing each part of the body, return to the chest and pay particular attention to the way it rises and falls. As you do this, you can also take this opportunity to fix your breathing.

Chances are that when you first notice your own breathing, you'll find that you are breathing in so that your chest expands first. But in fact, it should be your abdomen that moves first, and your chest should then follow this. Correct breathing, called abdominal breathing, should start by allowing the stomach to relax and protrude and then filling the lungs.

The process opens space in your abdominal cavity. This then allows the lungs to expand into that space, which is then followed by them expanding upwards through your chest as well.

This type of breathing allows you to take in more oxygen and trigger even more relaxation hormones. Most of us don't use this kind of breathing though because we have hunched postures which fold our stomach and prevent us from being able to breathe from there. The result is that we end up breathing with much shallower and faster breaths, which increases stress and cortisol.

But don't worry about that if you don't want to. For now, just notice your own breath and take this opportunity to count your breaths as they come in and out.

This is the part that is going to work a little like transcendental meditation by quietening down a lot of the activity throughout the brain.

**Step 5: Let Your Mind Wander**

Once you've done this for a little while and you're feeling still, it's time to just let go of your mind and let it do whatever it wants.

Here, your aim is not to control or silence your thoughts. Instead, you simply let your mind wander naturally–or stay completely still if it wants to.

The description that is often used is that you're watching thoughts go by like clouds. Headspace describes your thoughts in these cases as being more like cars on the road.

It emphasizes the importance of watching the 'cars' go past but not running out into the road to chase the traffic. It is all about detached observation.

After you have done this for a while, you can simply allow your mind to return to normal gradually and gently open your eyes.

Before we go any further, let's figure out how you can fit time for relaxation techniques into your daily life.

# Chapter 28

# Tips for Fitting Relaxation into Your Life

> "Within you, there is a stillness and a sanctuary to which you can retreat at any time and be yourself."
> - **Hermann Hesse**

RIGHT NOW, YOU MIGHT think, "I'd love to relax more and practice mindfulness. I just don't know how I'll fit it into my schedule."

You, like so many other people, spend so much time doing what you feel required to do that you think you already don't have enough quality time for anything else, including your family.

So, you ask, "How can I possibly find time to practice something like relaxation or mindfulness?"

That's a fair question.

Start by examining how you spend your days. To see what you can cut, ask yourself the following questions:

How much TV am I watching? More than an hour?

How much time am I spending on social media?

Could I be more efficient at work?

Can I drop some things from my schedule?

Can delegate some responsibilities to free up more time?

Keep track of how you spend your time for a week.

You might find that you are habitually spending time on things like social media or watching YouTube videos. There might be other ways you are wasting time without realizing it.

Getting rid of these timewasters can yield you some extra time you can use in better ways.

Once you've determined what you can cut, you can map out a plan to include relaxation and mindfulness practice into your schedule.

While there are no hard, fast rules, here are some things to consider as you contemplate how to fit a relaxation session into your daily life.

- Think about your schedule. Set aside a time in your day when you know you can fit in five or ten minutes to practice.

- This can differ, depending on your lifestyle. Some people find the first thing in the morning a good time before the day gets hectic. Others prefer to practice in the evening while winding down from a busy day.

- Many people find they can practice while they are doing other things. For example, you may relax and practice visualization while on the bus traveling to work. You can also practice mindful meditation walking after lunch.

- Remember to not get discouraged if you find you haven't set time aside to practice for a few days. Just practice when you can.
- Once you start your practice, you will find it easier to continue as your body becomes more comfortable with relaxation.
- Attach your practice to something you routinely do. For example, traveling to work on the bus, washing the dishes, or brushing your teeth. We are creatures of habit, so attaching your practice to something you do regularly already may help you remember.
- Do not practice relaxation when you are feeling sleepy, unless you want to go to sleep. To get the most benefits from your practice, wait until you are feeling alert.

Establishing relaxation time in a busy world can be a challenge. However, investing time in yourself is essential for your sense of balance and mental well-being.

You must make a point to prioritize your relaxation and mindfulness practice time. Don't hope that you'll find time for it after you accomplish everything else on your busy schedule.

Instead, intentionally set aside some time every day for relaxation and mindfulness.

This is what you're going to do next with three daily mindfulness exercises.

# Chapter 29

# Daily Mindfulness Exercises

*"It stands to reason that anyone who learns to live well will die well. The skills are the same: being present in the moment, and humble, and brave, and keeping a sense of humor."* - **Victoria Moran**

EVERY DAY, IT'S SO easy to get caught up in the stress and hustle of modern life. But you can take a moment every day to practice mindfulness and connect with your inner self. Three simple exercises you can do are mindful eating, mindful movement and sitting meditation.

**Mindful Eating**

Mindful eating is a great way to stay present in each moment. It involves sitting at a table and eating without engaging in other activities.

Don't talk, and there should be no TV, radio, book, newspaper, music, etc. Enjoy every bite with no distractions or judgment.

Pause and savor your food. Notice the colors, smells, and textures. Pay attention to how you cut it, the muscles you used to raise it to your mouth as you chew it slowly.

It will surprise you at how different food tastes when eaten in this manner and how filling a meal can be.

**Mindful Movement**

Mindful movement is also a great way to be present in the body. It can be a deep form of meditation if you approach it with full awareness.

In mindful movement, you strive to be aware of each step you take and everything that takes place around you.

Try walking while focusing on the rhythm of your breath and savoring the sensation of your feet touching the ground. Tune in to the sensation of your breath as you move while holding different postures.

Appreciate the surrounding beauty - the trees, birds and sky.

Try to become aware of emotions and thoughts that arise. Notice them then shift your awareness back to your body.

While stretching, be mindful of what it is out of your comfort zone, meaning where you felt uncomfortable. Discover what being in this uncomfortable zone feels like.

As you do this, you will also learn tolerance.

**Sitting Meditation**

Finally, sitting meditation is another wonderful practice that helps bring stillness and calm into our lives. This is simply being mindful of your sitting position.

Sit comfortably in a quiet space, close your eyes, and focus on the feeling of your breath rising and falling in your body. Feel your connection to the present moment and find peace within yourself.

While seated, imagine yourself as a mountain: grounded, stable, beautiful, and dignified.

Ensure that your hips are several inches above your knees by sitting on a pillow or a cushion, and your back is as straight as possible.

Remember to breathe!

Daily life exercises like these can help you cultivate greater awareness and insights about yourself and your life. By incorporating these simple activities into your daily routine, you will soon experience their calm-inducing effects and gain insight into yourself.

Now that you have these daily mindfulness exercises, let's look at another one you can use daily - body scan meditation.

# Chapter 30

# Body Scan Meditation

*"Mindfulness is a pause–the space between stimulus and response: that's where choice lies."*–**Tara Brach**

THE BODY SCAN IS a simple but effective way to bring mindfulness into your everyday life.

Mark out at least 30 uninterrupted minutes for this practice in a place where you can do this undisturbed. Make sure the place you choose is pleasant and comfortable and one where you feel safe.

Remember, you have set this time aside for you - to be with yourself.

Turn off all your electronic devices or - better yet - don't bring them into this space with you.

Now that you are in your space, just be mindful of being with things as they are in this place at this moment.

Let go of any preconceived ideas or thoughts of self-improvement or wanting things to differ from how they are.

Allow everything to be exactly as it is right now.

Just allow yourself to be as you are. Don't try to do anything.

Let your body be as it is. Just be aware of your experience and, as you become aware, do whatever feels right for you.

While it is safe, if you experience any feelings you can't cope with during the body scan, stop and get advice from a mindfulness teacher or a mental health professional.

Let yourself be open to any feelings and/or sensations that appear and allow them to come closer to you. This will give your feelings an opportunity to communicate what they need to with you.

Here are some guidelines to use for the body scan exercise:

- Kick off your shoes. Wear loose clothing, especially around your stomach and neck.
- Sit comfortably or lie down and close your eyes.
- If you lie down, you can lie on the floor, a bed, a mat or whatever feels comfortable to you. Keep your arms close to your side with your palms up and legs comfortably apart.

Put a pillow under your knees to make you feel more comfortable.

When you are still for an extended period, your body temperature can drop, so you may need a blanket to protect yourself. You will need to experiment to discover what works best for you.

- Notice the weight of your body on the mat, bed, or chair and the contact points between what's supporting you and your body.

As you breathe out, allow yourself to sink deeper into whatever is supporting you.

- Notice the sensations of your breath as it goes in and out of your nostrils, passing through your throat, or feel your belly rising and falling.

Just allow yourself to be aware of your breathing for a little while.

Now you're going to shift your awareness slowly to different parts of your body. As you do this, focus your attention on the sensations in each part of your body–be it the sensation of pressure from the floor beneath you, or the feeling of the air on your skin.

- Notice the sensations you have down your left leg.

Scan your left leg down past your knee, through your calf and shin, through your ankle and down to the tip of the big toe of your left foot.

Be curious about the sensations that appear in your big toe.

Is it warm or cold?

Do you notice your socks, or the movement of air?

- Now expand your awareness to your second toe, your third toe, your fourth toe and down to your little toe.

What do they feel like?

Don't worry if you don't feel anything special, just note the lack of sensation.

- With each breath you take, imagine it going down your body and down to the tips of your toes.

With each exhale, imagine the breath going back up your body and out of your nose.

- Use this same technique to allow your breath to move into and out of every part of your body as you pay attention to only to them.

- Now notice the feelings in the sole of your foot. Allow yourself to focus on the ball and heel of your left foot.

  Feel the weight of the heel sinking into the bed or mat or the floor.

  Notice the feelings on the sides and the instep of your foot, your ankle.

  Now breathe into the whole of your left foot and just let go.

- Go through this process of awareness with the lower part of your left leg, your knee, and your thigh.

- Notice any differences in feelings between your left leg and your right leg.

- Now allow yourself to notice the feelings in your right leg.

  Go down your right leg, as you did with the left, down to the toes in your right foot.

  Allow your awareness to move up your right leg as you did with your left, and then just let it go.

- Now gently place your awareness onto your pelvis, your hips, your buttocks, and your sexual organs.

  As you breathe into them, imagine you're filling them with an abundance of nourishing oxygen.

- Move your awareness up to your lower torso, your lower abdomen and lower back.

  As you breathe in and out, notice the feelings in your lower abdomen.

  Notice any emotions you feel here. If you feel emotions, explore them and accept them if you can.

- Now notice the feelings in your chest and upper back.

  Notice as your rib cage rises and falls with your breaths.

  Notice the beating of your heart.

Allow yourself to feel grateful that these vital organs are working in harmony for your highest good.

Be mindful of any emotions arising from your heart area.

Try to notice any emotions that arise and try to determine what they mean to you.

Allow yourself to fully experience these sensations without judgment or criticism.

Don't worry if thoughts or distractions arise.

Simply acknowledge them and then let them pass away as you refocus on your body.

With practice, you will eventually become better at recognizing when your mind has wandered, and more adept at bringing yourself back to a state of mindful presence.

Over time, this exercise can help to reduce stress and increase calmness, both mentally and physically.

Now, let's look at how you can use guided and non-guided visualization to enhance your mindfulness practice.

# Chapter 31

# Guided and Non-Guided Visualization

> *"Visualization is the act of willfully forming mental images. To affect material reality using visualization, form images for your subconscious mind to use as patterns to work from."* - **James Gor Jr.**

FOR THOUSANDS OF YEARS, people from all walks of life have used visualization to inspire and motivate them. It uses the power of your subconscious mind to help you harness the power of your unconscious.

Spiritual and energy healers have used it for many purposes, including to help fight cancer and reduce symptoms of cancer and cancer treatment. They also used it for many other maladies, both physical and mental.

One of its uses is to help your conscious and subconscious minds relax. The simple act of visualizing calm can help quiet the mind.

This helps to bring about a relaxation response which counterbalances any emotional distress you may be experiencing.

Like all other mindfulness practices in this book, visualization relaxation is a skill that you can learn. Like all skills, the more you practice, the better you will become.

You can practice either guided or non-guided visualization. Both can be highly effective in helping you relax.

## Guided Visualization

People use guided visualization to help them connect with something in their mind. It is a meditation or mindfulness technique where a person uses their imagination to create mental pictures, smells, textures, sounds, and feelings.

They can use these sensations to connect with a feeling, such as self-confidence or calmness. They can also use visualization to visit a place, like their favorite beach, or develop an action plan for a goal.

For centuries, people used this type of mental imagery to help them overcome a variety of illnesses. Over the past few decades, it has widely developed in not just psychotherapy but in many other healing modalities as well.

Guided visualization is a mental technique that stimulates your mind to produce mental images or memories. The wonderful thing about guided visualization is it can help a person control their thoughts while remaining in the present.

For example, if you are anxious because of an upcoming meeting or event, guided visualization can help you develop a plan to navigate that stressful situation.

Anyone may find guided visualization helpful.

In guided visualization, it is important to use a scenario that takes you to a place that you would normally feel relaxing.

In this example, we are going to use beach visualization.

**Procedure**

- Sit in a supportive chair or lie on your back and get comfortable
- Ensure your body is relaxed by releasing any areas of tension and allowing your arms to go loose, followed by your legs.
- Allow your arms and legs to become limp and relaxed. Let your neck, back and shoulders relax and let go of any tension.
- Breathe in and out, slowly, and deeply.
- Feel your body releasing any tension with each breath you take. Let your whole body become relaxed and peaceful and your mind calm.
- Feel a wave of relaxation flow throughout your body. Let go of any tension in any areas of the body that are still feeling tight.
- Now imagine you are walking toward the beach. You can hear the waves lapping on the shore and smell the ocean spray. Feel the warm air soothing your face.
- As you get closer to the beach, you can see the beautiful aqua color of the ocean ahead of you. Watch as the ripple of the waves glistening in the sun.
- The sand under your feet feels like soft powder, caressing your toes with its warmness. The beach feels fresh and soothing.

- Smell the scent of the clean saltwater entering your nostrils.
- As you breathe in deeply, inhale the fragrance of the smells.
- Here you feel a sense of freedom flowing through you. Your body feels completely relaxed and your mind is calm.
- As you approach the water, it washes over your feet. The cool water feels refreshing and is a welcome relief from the hot sand.
- You walk further out into the water. As you do, you're feeling fully refreshed and rejuvenated from the coolness of the water.
- You walk back to the shore and lie down in the sand, allowing your body to sink into the soft warmness.
- You feel completely relaxed as you soak up the warm sunlight as it caresses your skin.
- You are feeling calm and refreshed.
- All your stresses seem to have melted away
- When you feel ready, slowly make your way back up the beach. Find the pathway that you came on. You're slowly coming back to where you are today.
- Bring yourself back to your usual level of alertness.
- Let yourself keep the feeling of calm and relaxation that you gained from your practice.
- Open your eyes slowly, stretch your arms and legs. Becoming fully aware of your surroundings again.
- You are feeling refreshed and energized.

You can practice this visualization relaxation as often as you wish whenever you need it.

## Non-Guided Visualization

Like guided visualization, non-guided visualization can help you create mental images in your mind and relax.

The following is a quick way of getting away from a situation without physically leaving.

**Procedure**
- Imagine yourself walking towards a closed door in front of you.
- Open the door and walk down the 3 steps. Take in and let out a deep breath for each of the steps.
- When you get to the bottom of the steps, you walk into an environment where your body feels relaxed and your mind calm. This could be a familiar place, a happy memory, or a place from your dreams.
- As you walk around:
- What do you see?
- What can you hear?
- What do you smell?
- What can you touch?
- Spend a few minutes in this place, enjoying the feeling of deep relaxation.
- When you feel ready, make your way back up the steps, taking in and letting out a breath for each of the three steps.
- Make your way back through the door and back into the present.

As I hope you can see, visualization, whether guided or non-guided, can be another wonderful way for you to use mindfulness to create the life you want.

There are many more activities you can use to enhance your mindfulness. The next one we'll look at is mindful breathing.

# Chapter 32

# Mindful Breathing

*"Breathe. Let go. And remind yourself that this very moment is the only one you know you have for sure." –*
**Oprah Winfrey**

MINDFUL BREATHING IS A great way to take a break from work and get back into the present moment. It focuses your attention on your breath, which can help pull your attention back as it wanders.

If you only have a few minutes, mindful breathing can do wonders for getting your mind back into the moment.

Here's a ten-minute mindful breathing exercise you can do nearly anywhere:

Make yourself as comfortable as possible. It doesn't matter if you are sitting up in a chair, cross-legged on the floor, or even lying down on the couch or on a bed.

If you are sitting, try to keep your spine straight (only if you can - if you can't, find a position that works for you).

Once you find a place where you feel comfortable, just let your attention linger there.

Close your eyes and take a deep breath in through your nose, counting to three while you inhale.

All you are doing here is experiencing whatever is going on in the moment.

During this time, which is your time, you aren't trying to DO anything.

Just allow things to BE as they are, the best way you can, staying in the moment.

Feel your chest and stomach expand as the air fills you up, then count to three again as you slowly exhale through your mouth.

Feel the sensation of your breath going in and out of your nostrils, or up and down your throat.

Notice your belly rising and falling as you inhale and exhale.

Continue this pattern, focusing solely on each breath.

As thoughts enter your mind—like worries about work or what you're going to make for dinner later—acknowledge them, but try not to attach too much attention to them.

Try to let them go.

When your mind wanders away into thoughts, ideas, and plans, just notice it as it wanders.

It's okay when it wanders. It doesn't matter.

Acknowledge it and then bring your attention gently back to your breathing.

Every time you notice it wandering, just acknowledge it. It's perfectly normal and absolutely fine, just smile and bring your attention back to your breath.

Just gently guide your attention back to your breath without criticism. After all, it's simply part of the process.

Continue to breathe in and out, gently, and rhythmically.

The key here is to focus on your breath, allowing yourself to just observe without judgment.

With each breath, allow your body and mind to sink deeper into relaxation.

Continue this practice for ten minutes, focusing on the sensation of your breath as it moves in and out of your body.

When your mind wanders, simply bring your attention back to the sensations of your breath.

After ten minutes, slowly open your eyes and take a moment to observe how you feel. You may notice that you feel more at ease or relaxed than before.

Taking even a short amount of time to focus on your breath can help reduce stress and leave you feeling calmer and more relaxed.

This exercise will not only help you reset your mind throughout the day, but you can practice it anytime you need a moment of calm or clarity.

So next time you're feeling overwhelmed, try it!

There are many more activities you can use to enhance your mindfulness. The next one we'll look at is progressive relaxation.

# Chapter 33

# Progressive Muscle Relaxation

*"The is a secret for greater self-control, the science points to one thing: the power of paying attention."* - **Kelly McGonigal**

ALSO KNOWN AS "BODY scan" meditation, progressive muscle relaxation is a process where you pay attention to your body by tensing and relaxing different muscle groups in your body to relieve tension and induce a relaxation response.

By focusing on tensing and relaxing muscles individually, you focus on the present moment. Like all mindfulness practices, if your attention wanders, you refocus again.

Progressive muscle relaxation encourages mindfulness. When you combine progressive muscle relaxation with deep breathing, it is effective for relieving stress.

**Procedure**
- Take off your shoes, loosen your clothing, and get comfortable
- Find a quiet place.
- Sit in a chair or lie down on the floor or a bed.
- Close your eyes.
- Keeping your mouth closed, inhale through your nose, deeply and slowly.

Exhale slowly through your mouth.
- Repeat these deep breaths three or four more times. If it causes dizziness, breathe normally instead.
- On the fifth inhale, squeeze your muscles in your right foot.
- Count to four.
- Exhale slowly through your mouth, gradually releasing tension from your right foot.
- Imagine tension leaving your body.
- Incorporate a positive affirmation
- As you notice how you feel, say a simple affirmation like, "I am safe. I am comfortable. I am at ease."

You can do this either out loud or in your mind.
- Continue tensing and relaxing your muscles, using the following sequence.

1. Right foot
2. Left foot
3. Right calf
4. Left calf
5. Right thigh
6. Left thigh
7. Hips and buttocks
8. Stomach

9. Chest
10. Back
11. Right arm and hand
12. Left arm and hand
13. Neck and shoulders
14. Face

If you are left-handed, you can begin with your left foot instead.

When you finish the exercise, be still for a while and notice how it feels.

This exercise can be especially helpful if you are having trouble falling to sleep at night.

Let's look at one last exercise, mindful walking.

# Chapter 34

# Mindful Walking

*"Do not dwell in the past, do not dream of the future, concentrate the mind on the present moment."* —
**Buddha**

WALKING IS SOMETHING MOST of us take for granted.

If you're like most people, when you walk, you do many things.

Walking is so easy that you probably walk with your mind on automatic pilot most of the time. Since walking happens so automatically, you can build negative habit patterns that accompany your walking.

You might walk and talk on your cell phone, walk, and think about work, walk, and plan a vacation, or, like many people, walk and worry.

You might walk lost in thought or trying to figure out how to deal with the million-and-one tasks life imposes on you.

This doesn't allow you to pay any attention to the joy of being able to walk, walking itself.

This makes sense because walking is usually a DOING exercise. You are normally walking to get somewhere.

But what if you could find joy and appreciate the simple pleasure of walking?

In walking mindfulness, your goal is not to get anywhere, it is just to walk. This allows you to enjoy the journey, which is what mindfulness is all about.

Mindful walking is about slowing down, being present, and appreciating the act of putting one foot in front of the other. It's a chance to focus on each step - and on the world - rather than getting lost in your thoughts or dwelling on your problems.

It's a way to connect with the environment, no matter where you are, and it's an opportunity to be mindful of your body and the sensations it experiences.

So, take a moment to stop and notice the surroundings as you walk. Notice the trees in the park, the sound of your footsteps on the pavement, the feel of the wind on your face.

Allow yourself to just BE. Experience the world around you in its fullness.

Learning to walk mindfully can be transformative and open up an entirely new way of engaging with the world–all from taking a few steps.

## Walking Mindfulness Exercise

Set aside some time to just walk at a pace where you feel comfortable.

When you first practice, practice in your home or outside in your yard.

Your practice can be 10 or 15 minutes, whatever you feel comfortable with and have time for.

Walk at a very slow pace. As you do, here's what to pay attention to:

• Find your center by standing upright, as though a string is pulling the crown of your head up into the sky.

Your hips should be directly under your head.

You can find your center by leaning gently to the left and right, forwards, and backwards, until you find a balanced posture.

• Keep your knees slightly bent and your face relaxed
• Let your arms hang naturally.
• Feel your feet firmly rooted to the ground as you stand relaxed.
• Notice your breathing.

As you inhale and exhale, notice how it feels. Let your breaths fill you with joy.

• As you lean onto your left foot, notice how the sensations in your body change.

• Now shift your weight onto your right foot and note how the feelings change.

• Slowly shift your weight onto your left foot. Remove most of your body's weight from your right foot.

• Now ease your right heel up off the ground and leave it there momentarily.

As you do, just notice the sensations you feel.

• Now lift your right foot up off the ground. Put it down slowly, gently, heel first in front of you.

Allow your awareness to notice the weight of your body as it shifts from your left to your right foot.

- Now allow your right foot to rest slowly and firmly, completely on the ground.
- Continue to walk this way, shifting from one foot to the other and as you do, notice how your weight continues to shift from left to right.
- Continue walking in this slow, mindful way for the time you set aside for yourself.

This new form of walking can be a significant source of joy and peace.

As you practice walking mindfulness, notice the feelings that arise within you.

Feel gratitude for being able to walk. Marvel at how natural the movements of your body are. Appreciate the beauty that surrounds you.

Slow down and take time to fully immerse yourself in your surroundings. This can help put life into perspective and may even provide an opportunity for some introspection or spiritual exploration.

So next time you're out for a walk, instead of focusing on getting from point A to point B, try walking mindfully to really experience the fullness of each moment. Let go of any expectations, worries, or anxieties that weigh you down and give yourself permission to just be.

Enjoy the journey!

# Chapter 35

# Conclusion

"Be mindful. Be grateful. Be positive. Be true. Be kind." - **Roy T. Bennett**

MINDFULNESS IS NOT JUST being aware for its own sake.

It is an intentional and wise awareness of the world and of the workings of our minds so that we can recognize which habits are causing us unhappiness.

The awareness we are interested in is one that eliminates needless suffering by cultivating insight into the material world and the workings of the mind.

By learning to observe and accept your thoughts, feelings, sensations, and emotions without judgment, you can uncover your true self and learn how to cultivate a life of contentment and joy.

You discover how to respond in a way that is compassionate and mindful of others. This newfound awareness can help you manage your stress levels and make better decisions that benefit you and those around you.

But mindfulness isn't just about awareness. It's about action.

It encourages you to take responsibility for your life and to make choices that align with your values. Through mindfulness, you can learn to stay present in every moment and find beauty and joy in the here and now instead of relying on external sources of happiness.

Mindfulness might not guarantee happiness, but it provides a solid foundation upon which you can build the various elements needed for contentment.

You don't have to wait for the perfect moment to practice mindfulness. The time is always now!

I invite you to consider the challenge of taking up this practice and how it might change your life, just as it did for me.

With an open heart and mind, taking one step at a time, I'm confident that you will find in mindfulness a source of insight, presence, and even joy.

Why not try it and see for yourself what a difference it can make?

# About the Author

FEEL LIKE SOMETHING IS missing from your life?

Wil Dieck can provide you with the unique tools and teachings you need to unlock your full potential.

Wil is a master hypnotherapist, NLP and mindfulness Trainer and martial arts instructor who knows how to help his clients make the most of their personal and professional goals. With forty years of experience, he can show you how to use Mindful Mind Hacking techniques to strengthen your focus and create lasting habits of success.

Whether it's through his books, online courses, individual coaching sessions or group presentations, Wil will teach you how to break through any barriers that have been holding you back and start living the life you've always wanted.

So, what are you waiting for?

Get ready to reach and achieve your goals.

It all starts now.

Don't wait any longer.

Join Wil and start building the future you deserve!

Connect with Wil at mindfulmindhacking.com.

# Other Books by Wil Dieck

THE SECRETS OF THE Black Belt Mindset: Turning Simple Habits Into Extraordinary Success

Mastering the Mind, Body and Spirit: Secrets of Black Belt Peak Performance

Subliminal Success: How to Harness the Power of Your Subconscious Mind

Mindful Mastery: Find Focus, Get Unstuck, and Drop Into the Peak Performance Zone

NLP - UNLOCK YOUR DREAMS: A Beginners Guide to Neuro Linguistic Programming

1. https://www.mindful.org/what-is-mindfulness/

2. https://www.nature.com/articles/s41562-021-01093-w
   Nature Human Behaviour Article Published: 19 April 2021: A systematic review and meta-analysis of psychological interventions to improve mental wellbeing: Joep van Agteren, Matthew Iasiello, Laura Lo, Jonathan Bartholomaeus, Zoe Kopsaftis, Marissa Carey & Michael Kyrios

3. J Med Assoc Thai. 2013 Jan;96 Suppl 1:S90-5.: Effects of mindfulness meditation on serum cortisol of medical students: Wanpen Turakitwanakan 1 , Chantana Mekseepralard, Panaree Busarakumtragul

4. https://www.thelancet.com/journals/lancet/article/PIIS0140-6736(14)62222-4/fulltext

   The Lancet Articles Volume 386, ISSUE 9988, P63-73, July 04, 2015 Effectiveness and cost-effectiveness of mindfulness-based cognitive therapy compared with maintenance antidepressant treatment in the prevention of depressive relapse or recurrence (PREVENT): a randomised controlled trial: Dr Willem Kuyken, PhD, Rachel Hayes, PhD, Barbara Barrett, PhD, Richard Byng, PhD. Tim Dalgleish, PhD, David Kessler, PhD, et al.

5. https://link.springer.com/article/10.1007/s12671-018-0902-7

Mindfulness volume 9, pages 1543–1556 (2018): On the Association Between Mindfulness and Romantic Relationship Satisfaction: the Role of Partner Acceptance: Gesa Kappen, Johan C. Karremans, William J. Burk & Asuman Buyukcan-Tetik

6. https://link.springer.com/article/10.1007/s11682-018-9858-4

Brain Imaging and Behavior volume 13, pages 366–376 (2019): Reduced interference in working memory following mindfulness training is associated with increases in hippocampal volume: Jonathan Greenberg, Victoria L. Romero, Seth Elkin-Frankston, Matthew A. Bezdek, Eric H. Schumacher & Sara W. Lazar

7. https://www.frontiersin.org/articles/10.3389/fpsyg.2020.01053/full

Front. Psychol., 26 June 2020, Sec. Cognitive Science https://doi.org/10.3389/fpsyg.2020.01053 : The Mediating Role of Non-reactivity to Mindfulness Training and Cognitive Flexibility: A Randomized Controlled Trial: Yingmin Zou, Ping Li, Stefan G. Hofmann and Xinghua Liu

8. National Library of Medicine, PMC 2020 Jun 1.: The effect of mindfulness meditation on sleep quality: a systematic review and meta-analysis of randomized controlled trials: Heather L. Rusch, Michael Rosario, Lisa M. Levison, Anlys Olivera, Whitney S. Livingston, Tianxia Wu, and Jessica M. Gill

9. National Library of Medicine, PMID: 21802619 PMCID: PMC3679190 DOI: 10.1016/j.cpr.2011.04.006: Effects of mindfulness on psychological health: a review of empirical studies: Shian-Ling Keng 1 , Moria J Smoski, Clive J Robins

10. National Library of Medicine Clin Psychol Rev . 2011 Aug;31: Effects of mindfulness on psychological health: a review of empirical studies: Shian-Ling Keng 1 , Moria J Smoski, Clive J Robins

11. Front Hum Neurosci. 2019; 13: 208.: The Effects of Different Stages of Mindfulness Meditation Training on Emotion Regulation: Qin Zhang,1 Zheng Wang,2,† Xinqiang Wang,3 Lei Liu,4 Jing Zhang,3 and Renlai Zhou1,3,*

12. PMID: 25846954 PMCID: PMC4526594 DOI: 10.3758/s13415-015-0354-7 Mindfulness training for adolescents: A neurodevelopmental perspective on investigating modifications in attention and emotion regulation using event-related brain potentials: Kevanne Louise Sanger 1 , Dusana Dorjee

13. Education, v137 n2 p149-156 Win 2016: Behavioral Impacts of a Mindfulness Pilot Intervention for Elementary School Students: Harpin, Scott B.; Rossi, AnneMarie; Kim, Amber K.; Swanson, Leah M.

14. Neuroimage . 2018 Nov 1;181:301-313.: Impact of short- and long-term mindfulness meditation training on amygdala reactivity to emotional stimuli: Tammi R A Kral, Brianna S Schuyler, Jeanette A Mumford, Melissa A Rosenkranz, Antoine Lutz, Richard J Davidson

www.ingramcontent.com/pod-product-compliance
Lightning Source LLC
Chambersburg PA
CBHW062108080426
42734CB00012B/2801